KU-629-130

Praise for

CHANGE
ENTHUSIASM

"Change Enthusiasm *is the book you need to read at every stage of
your career . . . starting from the beginning! Cassandra does an amazing
job of being authentic, engaging, informative, and practical with this
step-by-step guide to harnessing the power of emotions. So many gems
on how to be your best self and leader through any career change."*

— **Melissa M. Proctor**, chief marketing officer, Atlanta Hawks and State
Farm Arena and best-selling author of *From Ball Girl to CMO*

*"Thank you, Cassandra Worthy, for providing us all with the best
advice we will ever receive on how to be change enthusiasts. How to
navigate through any type of change in our lives and in our careers
positively. As our world pivots around us these days, so too must
we. Cassandra, in her own brilliant way shares her emotional and
humbling journey, and through this inspires us all to challenge
ourselves for the better and to tackle the life changing things that
will deliver lifelong growth and happiness. This is a must-read!"*

— **Sarah Alter**, president & CEO, The Network of Executive Women

*"Many people will benefit from reading this book and applying
the wisdom, insight, and authenticity of Cassandra's journey. Her
message will resonate with leaders everywhere. After serving 22 years
in the military, I really hope that this book makes it into the hands
of military leaders. I've learned that, for change to happen, you must
be willing to see a situation from a different perspective. Thank you,
Cassandra, for being vulnerable and sharing your journey.
So many will be impacted and forever changed!"*

— **Phyllis W. Newhouse**, entrepreneur, retired military senior
noncommissioned officer, mentor, founder and CEO of
Xtreme Solutions, Inc., and founder of ShoulderUp

CHANGE

ENTHUSIASM

CHANGE
ENTHUSIASM

**How to Harness the Power of Emotion
for Leadership and Success**

CASSANDRA WORTHY

HAY HOUSE

Carlsbad, California • New York City
London • Sydney • New Delhi

Published in the United Kingdom by:
Hay House UK Ltd, The Sixth Floor, Watson House,
54 Baker Street, London W1U 7BU
Tel: +44 (0)20 3927 7290; Fax: +44 (0)20 3927 7291; www.hayhouse.co.uk

Published in the United States of America by:
Hay House Inc., PO Box 5100, Carlsbad, CA 92018-5100
Tel: (1) 760 431 7695 or (800) 654 5126
Fax: (1) 760 431 6948 or (800) 650 5115; www.hayhouse.com

Published in Australia by:
Hay House Australia Ltd, 18/36 Ralph St, Alexandria NSW 2015
Tel: (61) 2 9669 4299; Fax: (61) 2 9669 4144; www.hayhouse.com.au

Published in India by:
Hay House Publishers India, Muskaan Complex, Plot No.3, B-2,
Vasant Kunj, New Delhi 110 070
Tel: (91) 11 4176 1620; Fax: (91) 11 4176 1630; www.hayhouse.co.in

Text © Cassandra Worthy, 2021

Project editor: Melody Guy • *Indexer:* Beverlee Day
Cover design: The Book Designers • *Interior design:* Nick C. Welch
Interior photos/illustrations: Zakiya Goggins

The moral rights of the author have been asserted.

All rights reserved. No part of this book may be reproduced by any
mechanical, photographic or electronic process, or in the form of a
phonographic recording; nor may it be stored in a retrieval system,
transmitted or otherwise be copied for public or private use, other than
for 'fair use' as brief quotations embodied in articles and reviews, without
prior written permission of the publisher.

The information given in this book should not be treated as a substitute for
professional medical advice; always consult a medical practitioner. Any use
of information in this book is at the reader's discretion and risk. Neither
the author nor the publisher can be held responsible for any loss, claim or
damage arising out of the use, or misuse, of the suggestions made, the failure
to take medical advice or for any material on third-party websites.

A catalogue record for this book is available from the British Library.

Tradepaper ISBN: 978-1-78817-914-0
E-book ISBN: 978-1-4019-6178-7
Audiobook ISBN: 978-1-4019-6179-4

"You can be and do anything you set your mind to in this life." – My Mama

To my family, my rock, my foundation, and my love: Richard, Tishanna, Theresa, Gilbert, and Lisa.

CONTENTS

INTRODUCTION

According to McKinsey & Company, 70 percent of major change initiatives fail. But why?

Businesses small and large are going through unprecedented change as our world and those who inhabit it continue to evolve making change—and effective change response—a business imperative. Yet leading change effectively and efficiently, nurturing strong organizational resiliency, and quickly responding to market disruption or shifts in customer demand is much easier said than done.

Generally speaking, businesses exist to meet the needs of their customers and clients. Business growth is the result of change: a growth metric (profit, number of customers, market share, etc.) changing to a larger version of itself. And it's in the process of that change that instability often resides, instability that can stall or thwart the desired change or growth. That instability is created through behavior. People choose how they will behave based on their beliefs. In times of high-stress change, those beliefs are often fueled by the most important tool of successful change adoption: emotion. This is where Change Enthusiasm becomes powerfully relevant.

Change Enthusiasm (noun): (1) the practice of harnessing the power of emotion to grow through change; (2) a growth mindset

Too often leaders overlook the role emotion—the natural gifts of our species—plays in change. When going through change, we tend to hold within any negative feelings regarding the change as we interact with management, peers, and direct reports so as not to seem resistant or a troublemaker.

So we are left to manage our emotions in oftentimes unproductive ways, such as venting with others at any chance we get or numbing them with excess food or alcohol. The truth of change is that it is *people* who make it possible—people and their willingness to embrace and make change a reality. The undercurrent fueling that willingness is emotion. Emotion is a powerful energy that either stirs up organizational instability and unrest through change, or fuels a cohesive and determined organization that is focused on ensuring change is adopted efficiently and sustainably. The difference is both the degree of intention and action that leaders use to acknowledge individual emotional energy as well as the tools they provide their people to harness the power of emotion to fuel growth *through* the change.

I wrote this book to improve the 70 percent change adoption failure rate. I wrote this book to drive meaningful change in the number of organizations getting change right, enabling the people within those organizations to truly grow through the change. This book is for my 27-year-old self when I was in the throes of a billion-dollar acquisition, a young engineer tasked with influencing culture change while struggling to go into the office every day. This book is for my 34-year-old self striving to remain sober, when I was a midlevel executive leading an organization through a complex acquisition while building her own company. This book is for *yesterday's* self, a full-time entrepreneur in the grind, working to grow and expand the global footprint of her consulting firm. I wrote this book for those past selves because they represent the individuals, leaders, executives, and entrepreneurs leading and experiencing change today. They represent that individual who is struggling to see any good within their changing circumstance. They represent that person looking for a ray of light in the darkness of change, transformation, transition, and disruption.

Change Enthusiast (noun): (1) one who is inspired to grow by harnessing the power of emotion; (2) one who trusts the fear, anxiety, frustration, anger, and/or grief that change brings to be signals directing them to their greatest growth opportunities; (3) one who practices Change Enthusiasm

I am proud to be a Change Enthusiast. I am proud to be a living example of what I've presented in this book—that when the mindset of Change Enthusiasm is embraced and practiced consistently, it will light a path toward lasting and fulfilled growth through even the most life-shattering changes.

MY STORY

As I felt the cuffs clamp around my wrists and a slight tug as the officer escorted me to the curb, the world as I knew it was slowly crumbling.

My relationship with change hasn't always been . . . *healthy*. Where to begin? I guess as all things must: the beginning. For as long as I can remember I've had an insatiable curiosity. As a child my mind was constantly humming with questions: What is fog? Why does pool water smell weird? Where does the sun go when it vanishes below the horizon? What do adults use protractors for? Why do I see lightning before I hear the thunder? The list went on and on. This made the relationship between science, math, and me the healthiest threesome one could ever imagine. I quickly discovered that these disciplines armed me with the tools to explore and understand these mysteries of life. They also guided my career aspirations.

Early career goals of becoming a meteorologist (I was terrified of storms and thought meteorology would enable me to stay one step ahead) quickly turned to pediatric neurosurgery after seeing Ben Carson receive accolades for being the first to successfully separate twins conjoined at the head. This was a dream I held from the fourth grade until sophomore year of university. In that nine-plus-year span, my curiosity for the world around me ran rampant in my classwork, friendships, travels, and athletics. But it wasn't until sophomore year in college—when I began questioning this long-held career vision—that I decided to turn that curiosity toward myself. One day, I sat with that little fourth grader within and asked her why. Why did she want to become a pediatric neurosurgeon? She responded quickly and assuredly:

I want to be highly paid and want for nothing.

I want to help people.

And I want to wear scrubs to work.

Though the goals still resonated with my 19-year-old self (perhaps with the exception of wanting to wearing scrubs), I could envision dozens of paths to achieving them that wouldn't require the 15 to 16 years of additional schooling and residency necessary to become a neurosurgeon. After much second-guessing and hesitation, I decided to change my major from biology/premed to chemical engineering. Upon making the decision, I assured that little fourth grader I could still land a very well-paying job. The fruit of turning that curiosity within was the first major inflection point in my life. Granting myself a bit of grace, I released my childhood dream of becoming a pediatric neurosurgeon. I had adopted a major change in my career path in a healthy way. Knowing I was capable of doing so would later serve as a bedrock foundation that navigating through significant change, though difficult, was possible.

Around the same time as I was shifting gears in my professional pursuits, I kicked off a brand-new career I hadn't exactly dreamed of: drinking. At first my drinking was the relatively "normal" college drinking at parties and celebrations. But as I struggled with being comfortable in my own skin and moving into adulthood, it became a frequently indulged and well-mastered hobby with growing importance in my life. This growth continued for many, many years, surprisingly enough, running in parallel to my professional growth.

Following graduation, I spent the next decade-plus working in corporate America, learning and growing in my professional career at a rapid pace. I excelled in every endeavor, thirsty to learn how to successfully navigate corporate culture, my insatiable curiosity fully unleashed. I learned how to apply foundational engineering principles to scale consumer packaged goods from lab scale to manufacturing scale. I traveled the world. I indulged in new cultures. I developed meaningful and lasting relationships. I learned the nuances of influencing up, down, and across an organization. I learned how to recognize and unleash the strengths of others to accelerate business growth. I created and honed my leadership brand. And though I experienced steep learning curves with early advancements and role changes, my relationship with growth and ultimately change didn't become truly challenged until I had been working for several years.

This challenge came during my first billion-dollar acquisition experience. I was originally employed by the parent company and transferred into the billion-dollar business it had acquired, charged with continuing to lead breakthrough innovation while integrating the parent company's tools and processes. To this day, it remains the most challenging experience in my professional life.

In those early weeks, I remember feeling tension up and down the hallways, in meeting rooms, in break rooms, in labs, and on the manufacturing floor. This tension was being created by an "us versus them" mentality harbored by a critical mass of the organization. Seemingly every attempt I made to improve and grow the business was met with doubt and judgment. Though I originally stepped into the organization ready to embrace working together as one team, that powerful and contagious us versus them mentality slowly began taking hold of my heart and mind. I was so frustrated at the end of nearly every day that I began actively looking for ways to transfer out of the business and even quit the company—a company I had not long before loved and envisioned contributing to for decades to come.

My drinking career had become just as advanced as my professional career. Wrought with frustration and anger, every evening I numbed out with beer, wine, mixed cocktails, shots . . . being picky has no place in a world of dedicated drinking. My attempts to cope with this major change in my work life were leading to increasingly unhealthy choices outside of work.

Gratefully, my intuition somehow managed to blast through the sea of vodka, Red Bull, whiskey, and beer, and encouraged me to seek perspective from one of my senior-level mentors. I sat with her and expressed all my grievances, how tough of a time I was having, and how seriously I was considering quitting the company. During that chat I said everything short of recommending she terminate my manager and a few others in the organization to enable me to have a better work experience. She let me vent for a while and then looked at me, her eyes filled with such compassion and sincerity, and said, "Cassandra, I want to offer you some advice. You can either get *bitter* or you can get *better*. It's *your* choice."

That pissed me off. Her words initially led me to believe she had no concern for me or any desire to put effort into keeping me in the company. I had no choice in the matter. I wasn't in a position of power or influence, *she* was. But over the next several days, as I repeated "*bitter* or *better*" over and over in my mind, I began developing a different perspective. Those two words inspired me into this idea that I had control and power over how I *chose* to experience life, including the time spent at work. It was after embracing this idea that I was compelled to cultivate a growth mindset. It was a mindset grounded in trust that my emotions signaled an opportunity to choose my *better.* I trusted that for every negative emotion experienced, I could choose a course correction, that course leading me into my best self. By striving to practice this mindset on a daily basis, I managed to excel in that position, and because of it I landed an opportunity to move closer to my hometown while remaining with the company.

Over the next several years following this transfer, though my drinking and professional careers continued to flourish, it was the drinking that really picked up speed. It was leading me to become somewhat complacent in my career. Though I did faintly hear the voice of intuition telling me there was something bigger out there for me, that there was a better way for me to share my natural gifts and abilities with the world, I didn't stay sober and clearheaded long enough to really listen and explore it. Well whomever or whatever that voice was working with, unbeknownst to me they were devising a way of getting me to listen whether I liked it or not.

On a beautiful fall evening, I went out drinking as I had done so many nights before in search of that kind of joy that always manages to slip right through your fingers as night vanishes and morning appears. In the wee hours of the morning, less than a quarter mile from my house, I saw the blue lights flashing. Minutes later, I found myself handcuffed in the back of a squad car. I didn't understand its magnitude at the time, but the night I was arrested for DUI was to be one of the most critical moments in my entire life.

That first night in jail passed. My day in court passed. The reduction from DUI to reckless driving passed. The additional court-ordered 24 hours in jail passed. I stayed sober through it all. With the love, support, and inspiration from my parents, both recovering alcoholics themselves, I made the decision to once again turn the power of my insatiable curiosity within, just as I had done before. In doing so, I was better able to understand my drinking, grant forgiveness to myself for how it had become the rule instead of the exception, and fully embrace sobriety. As soon as I did all of this, I was free. Literally and figurately. Free to transform. Free to change from the inside out. Free to let my truest self blossom. Free to begin consciously enrolling in the life I most desired. And that's exactly what I did.

That night, before I was arrested, I met a gentleman at the bar. He and I engaged in one of the most provocative conversations on life and its many mysteries I had ever had. We discussed the power of belief, the difference between religion and spirituality, and whether or not coincidence truly exists. It was the conversation I kept coming back to in the wake of my arrest, our shared words serving as a guiding light on my new path. After several months of sobriety, I decided to reach out to that gentleman, and I did so with my whole heart in pure gratitude. I'm sharing what I wrote (names have been changed to maintain anonymity) to put this slice of my life's journey into perspective:

"Hey Tim!

Hopefully you remember me. We met at a bar in Buckhead nearly a year ago. Well, that night changed my life and you played an integral part in the transformation. This serves as my thanks to you for the part you played in completely turning my life around. So, I'll get right into it . . .

About two hours after I met you, I found myself sitting in jail after being arrested for DUI. Now I'll tell you I've never had any major trouble with the law. First arrest. First time in jail. But I had had several 'fortunate' run-ins with the law as a result of my drinking:

Pulled over for driving the wrong way down a one-way while drunk (and let go)

Pulled over while drunk on the interstate (and let go)

Approached by the police the morning after blacking out behind the wheel and hitting two mailboxes in my neighborhood (ticketed for hitting an object)

All of these incidents only fueled my 'invincibility.' I never, ever thought I would get a DUI because I believed I could control my drinking. Only alcoholics or people with real drinking problems got DUIs and I wasn't an alcoholic.

Well after getting home from jail I was rocked. I couldn't sleep. After being awake for nearly 72 hours filled with worry, guilt, and shame . . . then finally shutting off the TV and lying in silence with my spirit . . . with my thoughts . . . I had an awakening.

Something willed me out of bed to 'write it.' I literally heard a voice inside me repeating over and over 'Write it. Write it. Write it.' My mind suddenly drifted to you and our encounter. You had told me there were no coincidences. And that message just kept repeating over and over again as I wrote. It was then, at 4:30 in the morning, I was compelled to pull up your interview on YouTube for your book. And in listening to your words, it was as if divinity was speaking DIRECTLY to me through you. Here are a few excerpts from my journal as I was living this vivid spiritual experience:

'Utterly amazing. Amazing Grace. I just listened to Tim's interview on his book and his thoughts about life, God, and Spirit and it was the exact message that I needed to hear right now. And I'm weeping thinking about how much love God must have for me to have put him in my life just before giving me this life lesson. Utterly amazing. It's all true. It's all real.

Tim talked about living a righteous life. How by living an unrighteous life you find it difficult to hear God. Just take the root of that word: RIGHT. Live right. When you're living right you feel it. You're connected. Before now I believe I was aware but I clouded it. I numbed it.

. . . there are no coincidences. Everything happens for a reason and I'm sitting here feeling that overwhelming sense of reason.'

I didn't completely embrace that I was an alcoholic that night but it started the spiritual awakening required to get there. I haven't had a drink since the night I met you. Today I sit here writing to you as a very grateful recovering alcoholic. I now embrace my alcoholism as part of who I am and that it's completely okay. I can't tell you the level of gratitude I have for knowing that fact.

These past months have been some of the absolute best of my life. My consciousness is no longer drowning but thriving. I'm writing more. I experience REAL connections with people and share them through my writing. I am living more and more in line with this life's true purpose of bringing joy to all. My relationships are richer. I'm hurdling forward on my spiritual journey. I have clarity and awareness and I actually experience and FEEL real joy every single day. I now experience that awesome Divine power that runs through me and all of life in such an amazing way each and every day.

So, thank you. Thank you for being such a willing vessel of the soul of the Universe. Thank you for being such a major part of this soul's awakening. I beg of you to keep walking in your light. Keep listening to that God, Energy, Love, Consciousness that guides you on your path. You've probably moved more waves of consciousness than you know. But I'll tell you this wave is grateful."

As the mystery of life would have it, during my first year of sobriety I went through my second billion-dollar acquisition, tasked with leading my organization successfully through the transition. So many emotions, now enabled to be *really* felt without the nagging and numbing accompaniment of alcohol, signaled me into opportunity after opportunity to choose my better. I not only had to manage learning how to live sober, but also how to successfully orchestrate transitioning an organization through a major acquisition. The growth mindset I had cultivated during that first acquisition experience came to my rescue. Every ripple of frustration, every heartbeat-skipping ounce of anxiety, every flame of anger served as signals, welcoming me into opportunity to become better. The more I lived the mindset, the bigger the opportunities signaled.

Seeing and sensing frustration, anxiety, and anger among my peers, managers, and direct reports, I was inspired to find a way to package this mindset in a way that it could be shared. I was inspired to deliver that package to anyone and everyone struggling while leading or experiencing a significant shift in their career. I focused on building a consulting firm and speaker brand with this message at its core. After a couple of years juggling my full-time corporate work with building my firm, I set out to share this message full time with millions of people all over the world. This book is a part of the journey.

HOW TO USE THIS BOOK

> *Knowledge isn't power until it is applied.*
> — DALE CARNEGIE

When I set out to write *Change Enthusiasm*, I wanted it to be the kind of book that not only shared unique insights but also invited its reader to *act* upon the concepts conveyed. This book is intended to be a guide, a playbook for anyone leading, influencing, going through, or embarking upon change in their work. For example, onboarding to a new job, dealing with a new manager, leading a division through a redesign, starting up a new business venture, or navigating employment termination. But these tools and concepts can be applicable across all aspects of life, both personal and professional. Part I: The Basics, is composed of the foundational concepts and themes of the Change Enthusiasm mindset. Part II: The Practical Application, reinforces these concepts with real-life examples while inviting you to apply them in your own life.

I've included exercises that are intended to be completed at your own pace.

Part III: The Advanced Application, focuses on those often-overlooked soft skills that are critical to leading others through change by design. I firmly believe the most important cog in any change operation is the leader or influencer of change. By arming you with both the practical *and* advanced applications of Change Enthusiasm, I will help you enable your personal growth and achieve success through any change. In final Part IV: The Integration, you will learn the tips, tricks, and guidance to successfully integrate Change Enthusiasm into your life for sustained growth and fulfillment.

This book is a journey. Expect to be challenged. Expect to be entertained. Expect to be provoked. Expect to be inspired. Stay open to the *possibility* of change happening within *you* somewhere along the way and enjoy the ride.

PART I

THE BASICS

AN INTRODUCTION TO CHANGE ENTHUSIASM

Have you ever felt frustrated enough to punch a wall after the nth rejection of your business idea? Have you ever felt so anxious after a change announcement at work that you've been unable to sleep, worried about what it might mean for you and your livelihood? Have you ever feared you didn't have the strength and fortitude to lead your team effectively through a change?

When I was working at Procter & Gamble where I led an innovation organization in its Duracell business, I walked in one morning to the news that the business was being sold to Warren Buffett to eventually join his Berkshire Hathaway portfolio. Grief hit me immediately. It was like a punch in the gut. This very grand career I had envisioned with P&G was suddenly and unexpectantly being ripped away. You see, P&G had become all I'd known even before graduating from university. I had interned there for two summers and had a full-time offer to join the company at its headquarters in Cincinnati prior to starting my senior year. I had worked for the company for 12 years holding leadership positions across several businesses. Thanks to P&G, I had traveled the world, developed strong, rewarding friendships, and integrated myself into the culture of the company. To put it frankly, I had greedily guzzled the Kool-Aid and enjoyed the taste. I was comfortable in my career. I had envisioned which of P&G's future businesses I would contribute to and what new regions I would visit. I had even created a salary projection chart for myself envisioning the number and timing of advancements and bonuses.

When I learned of the acquisition news, I grieved not only for the loss of the comfort I had come to know and love for more than a decade, but also for the loss of my professional dreams. I felt an overwhelming sense of loss, and I didn't know how I would get through the acquisition let alone lead my organization through it.

When change occurs, the first things we experience are emotions. These oftentimes visceral emotions can make us not want to get out of bed, off the couch, or out of the bar. But why? Why does emotion hit us like a Mack truck? And why does that Mack truck at times feel as if it has rolled on top of us, making it seemingly impossible to breathe, let alone move? More important, what do we do about it?

Research shows that emotion travels faster than thought. Social psychologists have found that emotional response to a given stimuli is milliseconds faster than cognitive response.[1] This makes emotion one of the fastest known entities in the universe. These lightning-fast reactions that bypass the rational brain center have been in existence since our species roamed the Earth more than a million years ago.

Imagine yourself as part of a hunter-gatherer community far before Jeff Bezos made way for Whole Foods delivery and Garrett Camp and Travis Kalanick made Uber Eats possible. You're roaming the African landscape with a small group to secure food for the coming months. Your target is an ancestor

---

1.   Emily A. Sterrett, Ph.D., *The Science Behind Emotional Intelligence* (Amherst, MA: HRD Press, 2014).

to the antelope, but you're well aware of dangerous predators. The leader of the group signals there may be prey in the area and to step lightly and ready your aim. As you do so, gently placing one foot in front of the other with a crude weapon loosely gripped in your hand, you hear a very deep growl from behind you that vibrates your entire rib cage. What hit you first? Fear, and its associated physiological responses, or thought?

I understand that mental exercise can only go so far given you're likely reading this sitting comfortably far from danger, but our hunter-gatherer ancestors are thought to have experienced an immediate *feeling*. That feeling triggered the well-known fight, flight, or freeze response despite not having a brain with the complexity we hold today. Their nerve signals would first reach the amygdala region of the brain, which helps to process emotion, bypassing any semblance of a rational brain. In other words, emotion would signal a complex chemical chain reaction and as a result, our ancestors were presented with an opportunity: be consumed by a predator or devise a way to escape. It was emotion that *signaled* the opportunity.

Similar to our ancestors feeling fear upon sensing a potential threat, today we find that change elicits emotion, which in turn signals opportunity—opportunity to grow and evolve. Without embracing emotion as a signal or invitation to opportunity and learning how to leverage it as a gift, these signals can get the best of us, leading to stress, disengagement, and decreased productivity in our work and personal lives.

The emotions of change are real, natural, and highly efficient. But how can we leverage the power of these emotions, this prized inheritance of our species, to become more effective in the face of change? Change Enthusiasm is a growth mindset that can enable those who practice it to do just that.

Below are the steps to help you recognize and harness the power of your emotion to grow through change.

Figure 1: Change Enthusiasm is a growth mindset that when practiced allows one to harness the power of emotion to embrace and navigate change effectively. The Change Enthusiasm growth cycle is a three-step practice of embracing emotion as a signal, exploring the opportunity presented, then making a conscious, productive choice toward better.

STEP ONE: EMBRACE NEGATIVE EMOTION AS A SIGNAL

At the time of the Duracell acquisition announcement, all I wanted to do was run and hide. I wanted to leave the office to escape that ever-widening pit of grief in my gut. I wanted my manager to pull me aside and whisper, "Don't worry Cassandra, this impacts everyone BUT you. You are safe. You will remain with P&G." Actually, I wanted to erase the meeting that had just happened from ever existing in the first place. I honestly didn't want the news to be true. I didn't want to feel what I was feeling.

Whether experiencing a big change in your work or leading your organization toward your change vision, recognizing emotion as a signal is the first step to practicing this growth mindset in your everyday life. In my work with clients all over the world I have had the honor and pleasure of helping Fortune 100 leaders who were struggling to lead major shifts in their organizations. I have guided individual contributors who were once so fed up with their management they nearly quit. I have motivated entrepreneurs who were nearly paralyzed with emotion, unable to take the next step forward after what felt like their 10,000th investment rejection. I've seen C-suite executives who were anxious about making an important change announcement because they were unsure of how efficiently the organization would be able to process and execute the change.

I'm grateful for every encounter because each one reinforced the lesson that emotion is a necessary part of thriving through change, and when used effectively it can promote growth in both the individual and the collective. These thousands of connections have revealed to me the five most common emotional energies that bubble up when we are going through significant change, transformation, disruption, and transition: fear, anxiety, frustration, anger, and grief. These signal (or growth-stalling) emotions of change are shown in Figure 1 and defined in the Glossary, including their relevance in the practice of Change Enthusiasm. These hold true whether you're creating, leading, or executing change. Take a moment to familiarize yourself with each as I'll reference them throughout the book. Nothing levels the playing field more quickly than emotion. It is a resource in infinite supply that is available to us all, no matter our title or tax bracket.

There is a stigma associated with expressing emotion in the workplace. We've all heard that in order to be a strong, well-respected leader with unclouded judgment you have to leave emotion at the door. I would argue that leaving emotion at the door is more of a detriment than a benefit to professional success. All too often when it comes to our professional lives, we shove our feelings deep within or ignore them altogether. Being seen as someone who is overly emotional carries a certain stigma—a stigma that may impact advancement or placement into high-visibility leadership roles.

That said, there are business cultures I've experienced firsthand that are more inviting and accepting of outward expression of emotion—places where emotion is viewed as a by-product of *passion*, with highly emotionally charged individuals rebranded as *passionate*. There are two grounding beliefs contributing to the fabric of these cultures: (1) when an individual brings passion into his or her work, emotion is understandably present; and (2) there is mutual respect for all employees. Emotionally charged outbursts targeted at another employee were not tolerated. But even within these cultures, when someone was described as "passionate," it was often accompanied with a wink, as if to communicate that was code language for "hotheaded asshole." The risk of the aforementioned stigma remained. It is because of that risk—being seen as a highly emotional individual—that many people ignore or hide their feelings instead. It's time we rethink this.

Ignoring or hiding feelings, especially those perceived as negative, is an immediate pitfall in our evolution because we aren't allowing the use of this infinite resource, this valuable inheritance. Emotions exist to serve. The question is, how do we allow them to serve us in the most productive way? Do we allow ourselves to *become* the emotion? Do we allow our conscious thoughts to continually bring our awareness toward growth-stalling emotions like fear or anger? Do we hold that emotion within until the physiological effects—loss of sleep, high blood pressure, headaches, thinning hair, or worse— begin to impact our health? That would be like turning a gift into a curse.

To make the most of these precious gifts of emotions, we must trust that they appear to serve our best interests. Emotions and the physiological responses that often follow, such as raised hair follicles, dry mouth, or tingling skin, serve to alert us—if we pay attention. They alert us that it's time to explore what's possible. They alert us into an opportunity.

STEP TWO: EXPLORE THE OPPORTUNITY PRESENTED

After we have felt the signal emotions of change, allowed them to exist, and embraced them as a gift, we are presented with an opportunity: Explore what's possible in that moment to **GROW** into *better* or **SINK** into that downward spiral toward *bitter*.

Imagine you've been working in your current position for just over three years. It's a first-level management position despite the fact that you stepped into it with four years of prior experience managing others at a different company. You decided to accept the position after trusting there was opportunity to grow. Things have been going well for the most part and you like the work. The feedback you've been getting from your manager and your peers has been really positive. The culture of the organization is that advancement from a first-level management position typically happens within three to six years. It's time for your annual performance review and you're prepared to share with your manager that you think you're ready for and deserving of advancement and would like to understand how you can work together to put concrete timing behind it. You've prepared key talking points, including how you've exceeded several expectations of your role over the past two years.

Today's the day. Performance review time. You're wearing your sharpest outfit and you look like a million bucks. You're ready for this promotion. And you know it. You step into your manager's office with the confidence of a lion and take a seat. But before you can even begin your pitch, your manager starts to speak in a solemn tone: "Listen. I know this is probably going to come as a shock, but I've got some difficult news for you today. As you know, the company has been working toward our productivity targets and as part of an aggressive plan to meet them, we had to make some really tough choices this past quarter. These include downsizing my organization. Unfortunately, your role is being impacted by this effort and will be eliminated effective at the end of the month. HR will be reaching out to you later today to discuss your severance package."

Now in all likelihood that news would shoot tingles down your spine all the way to your toes. Those tingles are the physiological response of emotion. And that emotion, a complex hybrid of anger and fear, might very well be accelerating into all-out panic. What you thought would be a fruitful discussion about advancement turned into news of you losing your job. In that moment, with the signal emotions of change racing through you, what do you do?

Perhaps the panic ensues once you've left your manager's office. You begin blaming and cursing her under your breath for not seeing the value you bring. You feel a tightness in your chest growing as your thoughts drift to what you will tell your family and how you will continue to provide for them. You feel lost. All you want to do is crawl into a deep, dark hole with a bottle of Jack Daniel's and never come out.

What if there were another way to navigate this type of disruption? What if you embraced those initial emotions shooting up and down your spine as signals? What if you embraced those feelings surging within as alerts? It's your time to grow or spiral downward. What if you knew your reality to be, no matter how lost and panicked you might feel in the moment, that you have options? What if you knew the emotions of change were signaling you into these options?

It is through the practice of the growth mindset of Change Enthusiasm that those what ifs become reality. Within the second step of this practice, you can learn to fully trust that your signal emotions are inviting you into an opportunity to grow, and then begin exploring that opportunity by listing options to maximize it. The goal being to identify those options that inspire *growth-sustaining emotions* of change: anticipation, joy, hope, excitement, and gratitude. Let's explore what this practice could look like through the example presented. What options might you have in this particular scenario?

Signal Emotion	Option	Resultant Feeling	Potential Consequence(s)
Anger	Reach across the desk and slap your manager across the face, then scream at the top of your lungs that she will never know your worth and you never liked the company anyway.	Short term: exuberance and satisfaction Long term: embarrassment, shame, and grief	Rejection of severance package Escorted off premises Dark shadow on your résumé Loss of a positive reference Jail time
Grief	Accept the news. Prepare questions for the HR meeting.	Short term: anticipation	Better understanding of severance package
	Read through all prior-year performance reviews. Begin summarizing what you've learned and how you've developed skill sets over the past three years. Draft an updated résumé.	Short and long term: gratitude	Updated résumé with an additional three years of rock-solid experience

Table 1: When experiencing the signal emotions of change, first recognize and allow them to exist. Then list options that will inspire growth-sustaining emotions such as gratitude, as well as potential consequences if the action is taken. In this example, we see what it would be like to move from anger to long-term embarrassment and shame, versus moving from grief to anticipation and gratitude.

You could probably think of several options that would bring about short-term satisfaction, but in the long term would not sustain growth and fulfillment. The best way for us to use the gift of emotion is to allow it to guide then fuel us through the productive choices that can enable our growth and betterment.

After allowing the grief and anxiety to exist following the Duracell acquisition announcement, I embraced the fact that I had been placed in a massive moment of opportunity. I began exploring *my* options.

Signal Emotion	Option	Resultant Feeling	Potential Consequence(s)
Grief	Accept the news. Research Warren Buffett. Research Berkshire Hathaway.	Anticipation	Better understanding of Berkshire as a company to contemplate whether I would like it to be part of my career Better understanding of what benefit this transition could afford my career
	Lament the loss of P&G. Find any way to remain with P&G.	Grief, Frustration	Be viewed as someone resistant to change Inspire feelings of frustration throughout my organization.

Table 2: Exploring options and the anticipated feelings and consequences if pursued.

Once I laid out these options, I felt empowered to take back control of my career through the power of choice.

STEP THREE: MAKE A CONSCIOUS, PRODUCTIVE CHOICE

The power of choice is immense. Where you sit in this moment is the result of a series of choices you have made that led you exactly here. There have been countless books written about choice, from what drives it to what's happening at a biological level when we are engaged in decision-making. But it is during times of change and transformation that the importance of leveraging the power of choice is unparalleled. It's no coincidence that choice is at the very center of the growth cycle in Figure 1. Our personal growth is a composite of lessons learned, wounds healed, and successes achieved. This is made possible only through conscious choice. Remaining healthy is made possible through *consciously choosing* what you feed your body and how you keep your body strong. Learning how to surf is made possible through *consciously choosing* to get up and try again after you fall. Building a track record of impactful leadership is made possible through *consciously choosing* how you behave or show up to your organization.

Change happens. Whether we bring it into reality or it happens without our having asked for it, it is up to us to choose how we embrace change to propel our growth. By doing the work of listing options when experiencing the signal emotions of change, which we'll work on in greater detail in Chapter 5, all that's left to do is employ this power of choice. For me that meant accepting that my business was being acquired and exploring next steps. That was my choice because it led me to a better feeling. It didn't immediately remove the grief, but it certainly put me in a mind space where I could begin engaging authentically and inspiring my organization through the acquisition. That looked like holding one-on-ones with direct reports solely focused on how they were managing the change and if I could support them in any way. That looked like using time during team meetings to express at least two things we could be excited about exploring in the new company. That looked like intentionally holding space for others to share thoughts and feelings regarding the changes and setting that same expectation of my manager.

Once you've created your list of options, consciously choose the most productive one, the one that inspires a better feeling. It's through consciously deciding to feel better and to become more productive that we pave the way for growth. I know what you're thinking: *It's too difficult to move away from those signal emotions!* And I agree, sometimes it feels as if the healing has to begin by just sitting with them. It often feels necessary for us to vent and commiserate with others on how much everything around us sucks, indulging in the instantly gratifying comfort of it.

I've been asked more times than I can count what to do when the signal emotions are so overwhelming you can't even remember what joy and excitement feel like. The truth is, there are times when the emotions of change hit you so hard that all you can seem to see is darkness: losing your job, not getting the promotion, getting told no for the nth time when trying to grow a business, or losing the company and culture you grew to love because of an acquisition. Regardless of where you are in your **change journey**, this growth mindset is still applicable. Because it's not about instantly jumping from frustration all the way to excitement. It's not about blind optimism and positivity. It's about consciously choosing what will bring about the *next-best* feeling. It's about choosing what will bring about a *better* feeling not the *best* feeling. And it's okay to allow the negative emotions to exist. They are gifts. Granting yourself time and space to sit with them is an important part of this process. Change Enthusiasm meets you exactly where you are. Just remember to allow those signal emotions to exist while trusting that they are there to serve, to invite you into your greatest opportunities to grow. Then when you're ready to go about the business of living this mindset, you'll reach better and better feelings through *conscious enrollment* in the evolution to your best self.

The more you practice this growth mindset, the more you will recognize every big change challenge in your life is not happening *to* you, it's happening *for* you. To serve your growth. To provide an opportunity to learn.

The acquisition by Warren Buffett meant my departure from P&G and subsequently joining the ranks as an employee of Duracell. It meant the close of a 12-year career with a company I loved. It meant the obliteration of my professional dream to end my career within the walls of P&G. Throughout the transition from being an employee in a P&G business to being an employee of a stand-alone company in the Berkshire Hathaway family, I felt the signal emotions of change more times than I could count, which resulted in numerous really tough days. But *because* of that experience I was able to clarify and crystallize the strategy of Change Enthusiasm. *Because* of that experience I know firsthand how to apply it to yield results. *Because* of that experience I founded a successful consulting firm that enabled me to travel the globe nurturing the world's resiliency, elevating conscious innovation, and inspiring conscious leadership through change. *Because* of that experience I am better prepared to relate to my client base. I know that acquisition happened not to me, but for me. To serve my growth. To enable me to make a conscious choice toward living a more purposeful life in service of others. This is what I call *20/20 change vision*.

Have you ever looked back on a change challenge such as losing your job or being turned down for a role you *really* wanted and recognized it to be the catalyst for something great? Have you ever embraced that event, what was seemingly a low point in life, as one of the best things that's ever happened to you? That's 20/20 change vision. It's when you can see how a change event that brought about what seemed at the time like unbearable signal emotions happened for a reason—so you could become a better leader, a better business owner, a better partner, a better parent.

Through practicing Change Enthusiasm, you are training yourself to have that 20/20 change vision not months or years after a change event but *while you're going through it*. It will no longer be *hindsight* vision created through evidence; it will be *present v*ision made possible through trust . . . through belief. Having this vision when going through a change event will become your competitive advantage, enabling quicker, conscious choice of better feelings and better results. You will become more and more enthusiastic about change, trusting that it means continued growth toward your best self. You will build an enviable strength of resilience.

RESILIENCE IS A MUSCLE

Have you ever met someone who always springs back up no matter how hard they get knocked down? And they do it with an exuberance and dedication unlike anything you've ever seen? So much so that it inspires you to do better? Becoming *that* person is the promise of Change Enthusiasm. When you can practice this mindset every day, through every change challenge, every disappointment, every failure, you will build your muscle of resilience. You will embrace the idea that every change challenge happens *for* you. You will quickly recognize the signal emotions of change as gifts serving your growth and betterment. You will become an inspiration to those around you.

Just as our physical muscles have to be stretched, torn, and ripped during training and exercise in order to rebuild themselves bigger and stronger, so does the muscle of resilience. We do this through the practice of experiencing change. Change wears many faces: rejection, failure, loss, triumph, and accomplishment. The more we can experience these faces of change and engage this mindset, the stronger our resilience will grow.

Picture two people—Individual A and Individual B—in the experience presented earlier of having been told they were being let go from their position. Consider the news of being let go as the *change event*. Individual A has been a practicing Change Enthusiast for a few months and therefore was able to quickly recognize their signal emotions, embrace the opportunity for growth, and choose the option that brought them closer to the growth-sustaining emotions of change. Individual B, however, lingered in the signal emotions, not making conscious, productive choices toward their better self.

The strength of your resilience muscle is directly related to how quickly you can recognize the opportunity that change presents and make a conscious, productive choice toward a better feeling, and a better result. The resilience muscle of Individual A is stronger than that of Individual B. The impact is reaching a better feeling and likely a better result sooner, thus creating a competitive advantage.

Armed with 20/20 change vision, Individual A chose the options of accepting the news, preparing questions for HR, and updating his résumé. Feeling better and better with each passing day through conscious choices, he sent out the updated résumé to dozens of people in his network. Shortly after the termination was effective with weeks left of severance pay, he got a call from a prior colleague who had received the résumé and sent it to the hiring manager of a position she thought might be a great fit. Turns out the hiring company had been at the top of the list of his dream places to work during his job search four years earlier. He was invited to interview and nailed it. It was *because* of the experience gained and the glowing reference his manager provided from the role in which he was just terminated that he shot to the top of the candidate list and was extended an offer, which he gratefully accepted. His acceptance meant a 20 percent increase in base salary with a comparable benefits package. He enjoyed several weeks of both severance pay from the old job and salary from the new one. He is now at a company he loves, doing work he thoroughly enjoys, having trusted all along that the termination happened to serve his growth.

Now in no way am I implying that Individual B didn't go on to land a great role. But if they had been vying for that same position at that same company, Individual A would be the one with the competitive advantage. In the game of change, it's not simply the early bird who gets the worm, it's the most resilient who truly feasts.

You will be presented with countless change events in your lifetime. With each comes the potential for those signal emotions: fear, anger, frustration, anxiety, and grief. Those emotions will never disappear; they are here to serve. Through the practice of experiencing change and Change Enthusiasm, your resiliency will grow, enabling both your personal and professional growth to accelerate. The more revolutions you make in the Change Enthusiasm growth cycle depicted in Figure 1, the better you will be able to harness the power of emotion to accelerate your growth.

The emotions of change are real and undeniable. Though tough at times, they serve as signals to our growth opportunities. As a leader, innovator, or entrepreneur, it is imperative to leverage the power of these emotions to enable growth and ultimately your ability to navigate change effectively.

In the pages that follow you'll learn how to apply both practical and advanced applications of this growth mindset in your own life. You'll learn how to build your resilience muscle, increase your emotional self-awareness, become a more effective leader, and ultimately harness the power of emotion to navigate change effectively and consciously evolve to your best self.

Chapter at a Glance

- Change Enthusiasm is a three-step growth mindset:
    1. Recognize growth-stalling emotions such as fear and anxiety as signals to grow.
    2. Embrace the opportunity change presents, exploring options that lead to your better.
    3. Make a conscious, productive choice, having explored what's possible, to transform emotional energy into fuel toward a better feeling and better result.

- The signal (or growth-stalling) emotions of change are fear, anxiety, frustration, anger, and grief.

- The growth-sustaining emotions of change are hope, anticipation, excitement, joy, and gratitude.

- Change presents opportunity to grow toward your better self.

- 20/20 change vision is being able to see clearly that major change, disruption, or transformation happens *for* you, to serve your evolution to your best self. It is a knowing and trust that opportunity to learn and grow lies within even the toughest changes and disruptions.

- Resilience is a muscle that is built through the practice of experiencing change, including any disappointment, failure, or rejection that may accompany it.

- When practiced on a regular basis, Change Enthusiasm becomes a growth cycle that helps strengthen your resilience muscle.

LASTING CHANGE IS ROOTED IN BELIEF

In mid-March of 2020, I traveled to three different metro-Atlanta grocery stores in search of toilet paper. As I rounded the corner of aisle 17 in that third store feeling exhausted, I saw what I knew in my gut would be true: barren shelves. This store too had been wiped out by anxious, frantic shoppers buying up as many rolls as they could fit into their shopping cart. My situation eclipsed desperation and, in that moment, became comical. I couldn't find toilet paper within a 30-mile radius of my house.

On March 12, 2020, former president Donald Trump addressed the nation from the Oval Office for just the second time in his presidential term. In a very serious tone, he shared details of the United States government's response to COVID-19, the disease caused by the new coronavirus. That same day the World Health Organization declared the virus a global pandemic. The next day, ironically Friday the 13th, Trump declared a national emergency to release approximately $50 billion of funds to assist with on-the-ground testing, treatment, and vaccine research. Within the course of that 48-hour period, the world I had known changed forever.

The headlines such as those from *Politico* magazine ("Coronavirus Will Change the World Permanently. Here's How.") and CNN ("US coronavirus: Now a pandemic, life for Americans has changed indefinitely") reinforced this.

You're probably picturing in this very moment a vivid mental image of where you were and what you were doing when the virus infiltrated your country. This is imagery that has been seared into our mind's eye. Our lives changed forever as a result of the coronavirus pandemic of 2020.

Why? Why were our lives altered indefinitely within those several weeks? Millions abided by shelter-in-place executive orders from their respective governments, self-quarantined for weeks on end. Schools and businesses closed their doors. Working remotely became the norm seemingly overnight. Parents had to juggle working while taking care of rambunctious kids home from school. Jobs were lost. Bills went unpaid. Government-funded stimulus efforts were introduced all aroundtheworldtosupportcitizensfacingeconomicshutdown. Trips to the grocery store caused never-before-experienced anxiety in many. Health-care systems all around the world were strained in unprecedented ways. Hundreds of thousands of loved ones perished in the U.S. alone. Countries came together to support one another like we had never seen before. These statements alone could be the supporting rationale for systemic change. But at a fundamental level, what was happening within our global community during this time exemplified on a grand scale the secret behind creating lasting change: Belief. *Belief* is the true driver of change because in order to achieve it, BELIEF must change.

WHAT HAPPENS *INSIDE* CHANGE?

All the world's a stage, and all the men and women merely players.

— WILLIAM SHAKESPEARE

To further explore the relationship between belief and change, let's break down the concept of belief through the lens of change. But first, a brief digression. Have you ever wondered why change is commonly represented by this symbol: Δ? The first time I pondered this was in my high school calculus class when studying derivatives. Thinking I had finally escaped geometry a few semesters prior, I wondered why I was suddenly looking at a geometric shape in my textbook. I learned the triangular shape is a delta, which is the fourth letter in the Greek alphabet. The core meaning is "difference." It is the difference, or *change*, in a certain quantity. This tiny symbol followed me throughout my academic career as I pursued a degree in chemical engineering. During my college years I enjoyed the symbol so much that I used it as shorthand for *change* in notes and e-mails that had nothing to do with coursework, which annoyed my friends and family to no end. I'm now tickled by the irony that my life's work is enabling others to grow through Δ.

Imagine the space within Δ as we consider the process within change, what change is made of, and ultimately this idea of belief being the key to creating lasting change in your life (*see Figure 2*).

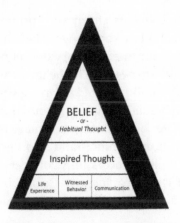

Figure 2: A look within the change delta. Foundational elements stimulate or inspire thoughts and emotions. The stronger their influence, inspired thoughts become habitual thoughts or beliefs, the keystone element of lasting change.

At the base, the very foundation of change, are elements that influence change: our experiences, behavior, and communication. See examples below:

Life Experiences	Witnessed Behavior	Communication
• Climbing a mountain • Eating ice cream for the first time • First successful bike ride without training wheels • Being arrested for DUI • Getting promoted • Being hired by Google	• Managers berating employees • Peers showing up to the office at 6 A.M. and being rewarded • CFOs stealing from the company with no reprimand or consequence • A vice president who shows up for every retirement party • Every new hire being given a welcome lunch • Masses of people buying toilet paper and paper towels	• Body language like eye-rolling, head-shaking, and deep sighs • Organizational announcements • Books • All-employee e-mails from CEOs • Netflix, Disney Plus, Apple TV, YouTube TV, and Amazon Prime shows • E-mails from managers • Press conferences

Table 3: Examples across the three foundational elements that can influence change: life experience, witnessed behavior, and communication (verbal and nonverbal).

All of these elements churn and inspire thought, flowing into the second layer of change. They invite us to create meaning in both our internal and external worlds. What we experience in life shapes us. The behavior we see in others informs how we should or *could* act in a given situation. The behavior and subsequent reward or consequence we witness in others motivates our behavior. Language makes it possible to learn new concepts, understand and become fascinated with Greek mythology, successfully complete a road trip from Atlanta to San Francisco, identify Orion's belt in the night sky, or install a spare tire. These three elements guide our way in life.

The Shakespeare quote at the start of this section of the book has always been a favorite of mine. As I have studied lasting change, it has had growing importance. It's a perfect analogy to life. Our experiences create the narrative, the plot of our life's story. The behaviors of others define the supporting cast. And what we digest through communication becomes a core part of the script.

As you sit there, can you think of a pivotal life event that has become part of your story? Something that happened and suddenly altered the telling of your life story to what came before and what came after? The coronavirus pandemic of 2020 for many, including myself, is one of those events. A time in life when what happened across all three foundational elements will continue to inspire thought for years and years to come. A time that became the foundation of lasting change by thought turning to belief.

DO THOUGHTS *REALLY* TURN TO BELIEFS?

What we think determines what happens to us, so if we want to change our lives, we need to stretch our minds.

— WAYNE DYER

Thought is our way of interpreting and making sense of the world around us. Every change foundational element invites us to create meaning from it and in doing so invites us to think. Everything finds its origins in thought: a cultural movement, breakthrough technology, top-charting song, an immaculately designed home. It all begins in the mind, growing from a seed of thought energy. When a given stimuli (life experience, witnessed behavior, and/or communication) is particularly strong it may inspire the same thought over and over. Once that thought becomes habitual it turns to belief, the top of the change delta.

Abraham Hicks, arguably one of the greatest teachers of our time, defines *belief* as "a thought I keep thinking." The classic definition of belief is "a state or habit of mind in which trust or confidence is placed in some person or thing." At first glance these definitions may seem different, but they aren't. Let's explore the classic definition. A *"habit of mind* in which *trust* . . . is placed." What creates trust? The thoughts we keep thinking reinforced by some combination of life experience, witnessed behavior, and communication. When one thought gets played over and over in our minds, it becomes habitual and in so doing transforms into a belief. The thought becomes the material by which the fabric of trust in someone or something is made.

Think of someone you trust more than anyone else in your life. That person you know you could call on for anything. That person you know will always be there when you need them. Picture their face in your mind's eye right now and ask yourself: *Why* do I trust them?

For me, that person is my brother Richard. I know that no matter what, if he is physically capable he will be there whenever and wherever I need him. I trust in him fully and completely. He is one of the most devoted people I know. My trust has been built by the countless times he's shown up for me. Car breakdowns in the middle of the night, he was there. Plumbing issues, he was there. A last-minute airport drop-off of something I forgot, he was there. A midnight phone call just to vent, he was there listening patiently and compassionately on the other end. With every behavior, experience, and communication the thought *he will be there for me* has been reinforced. As a result, that same thought has played over and over again in my mind thousands of times.

Those foundational elements of change have inspired habitual thought or belief in him. Belief in what he will do, how he will respond to a request for help. Habitual thought has become the fabric of the trust I hold in him. With hundreds of thousands of thought strands, that fabric now carries the strength of steel.

The thoughts we keep thinking create a mental web that holds us together. Our beliefs help us make sense of life. This is why change can be so difficult at times. Sustained change happens most often when an existing belief changes. It can also happen when a new belief is formed, but more often than not that new belief works in concert with an existing belief changing. The strength of a belief web lies in the thousands of thought strands from which it is created.

Every time we think the same thought a new thread is woven. Every experience, witnessed behavior, and communication has the potential to reinforce that thought, stimulating it to be replayed, rewoven. Think of how difficult it would be to tear a fabric made of thousands of threads. Our long-held beliefs are like that.

 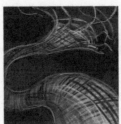 

They become our comfort, our warmth holding our sanity in place. Internal change requires our webs to change; threads must dissolve in order for new ones to take their place. This process takes much mental energy, devotion, and time. But it is when that shift happens internally that external change, the change others can see, manifests.

WHAT ABOUT EMOTION?

*I've learned that people will forget what you said, people
will forget what you did, but people will never forget
how you made them feel.*

— MAYA ANGELOU

At every level of change there exists the potential for
emotional energy. In fact, this energy is often the first thing
that hits us. Every experience. Every behavior witnessed.
Every book read, podcast heard, conversation had, and movie
seen. That emotional energy strengthens thought, accelerates
thought, and fuels action. Have you ever noticed how the
times when you have felt the highest levels of stress or the
most extreme joy correlate to pivotal moments in your life?
I'll never forget sitting in the back of that squad car, handcuffed, being driven to jail. The guilt. The embarrassment.
The shock. The fear. That short ride changed my life forever.

In the chapters that follow we will discuss emotion and
change in a much deeper context. But for now, understand
that emotional energy plays a very important role in either
fueling or preventing lasting change.

HOW DOES BELIEF DRIVE BEHAVIOR?

*You know, a lot of us have always had challenges of changing
behavior, whether it's exercising regularly or different habits with
smoking . . . when it affects us. What's been remarkable to
watch here is how the American public has changed their
behavior when it protects the vulnerable. I think that's
really what I'm so proud to see.*

— ROBERT REDFIELD, FORMER CDC DIRECTOR

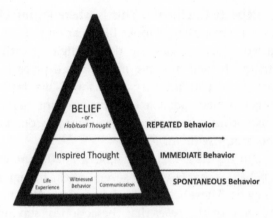

Figure 3: Every level of the change delta can lead to action. Those behaviors become repeated and habitual when rooted in a strongly held belief.

Spontaneous Behavior. These are the behaviors I have experienced in myself and observed in others to be anchored purely in the foundational elements of change and fueled by emotional energy. These are our knee-jerk reactions—when we *become* the emotion that a given stimuli incites within. When we *become* rage and storm out of a meeting. When we *become* grief and crumble to our knees. When we *become* joy and dance around uncontrollably. When we *become* fear and run down the street screaming. This will be discussed further in future chapters.

Immediate Behavior. These are the behaviors fueled by emotional energy and a heightened sense of urgency but anchored in some level of conscious thought. For example, you're at an amusement park and witness someone taking a big bite of a deep-fried Oreo cookie and it inspires the following thought: *Boy, that looks good. I bet it tastes good, too. I want one.* The resulting, immediate behavior is walking to the deep-fryer tent, purchasing a deep-fried Oreo, and enjoying one for yourself. Immediate behavior creates new life experiences that stimulate even more thought.

Repeated Behavior. This is where lasting change manifests. Lasting change looks like year-on-year profit declines turned into year-on-year double-digit growth, high-level attrition turned into the most desired place to work, or a start-up turned industry mainstay. This lasting external change is made possible once belief or internal change happens within organizations and the individuals and leaders who comprise them.

During the global pandemic of 2020 there were changes in behavior that lasted for several weeks in regions all across the globe. These behavioral changes lasted because they were anchored in the *belief* that the action of staying home and following social distancing guidelines would protect not only ourselves but the most vulnerable of the population and help to mitigate the strain on health-care systems and workers.

Lasting change happens when beliefs—or the thoughts we keep thinking—change based on life experience, witnessed behavior, communication, or some combination thereof and fueled by emotional energy. To exemplify, let's take my toilet paper example through the entire pyramid:

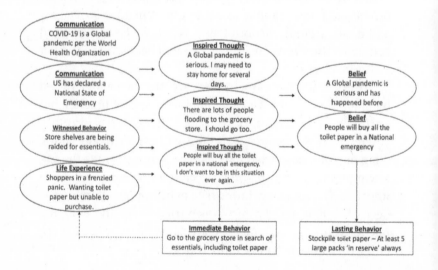

Entwined within it all was emotional energy, which served as fuel to every action. My thoughts made the emotional energy that much more apparent. When the next pandemic or global emergency strikes, I will not need concrete knowing that shelves are being raided to inspire a reaction of searching stores. Because I carry the belief that a pandemic can happen, supported by past experience, my repeated behaviors have changed. My relationship with toilet paper has forever changed. I now ensure a stockpile of at least five large packs at all times and often purchase two bundles at a time instead of one.

HOW DOES THIS RELATE TO BUSINESS?

All of my best decisions in business and in life have been made with heart, intuition, guts . . . not analysis.

— JEFF BEZOS

All too often I've heard that belief—or what you hold as a personal truth—has no place in business and should be left at the door. Talking about belief in the workplace is not politically correct. This may hold true regarding religious beliefs, but *belief* as we've just defined it ("thoughts we keep thinking") is a critical part of success for any and every business. It must exist and, quite frankly, can't help but. As we just learned, sustained change is made possible when belief changes. Therefore, belief holds an important place in business. It's just that in a business context it is often veiled in different language. We use words like *purpose* and *value*. A company's list of values is its communicated belief structure. These are the thoughts it wants its employees, clients, and customers repeating over and over in their minds when it comes to the business. And a belief system falters if the experiences, internal communication, and *behaviors* of the company's leadership are not congruent. A classic example of this is Enron, the American energy company brought down by a spectacular and very public scandal. Enron's value system was idealized as one of high integrity, but the behaviors of the leaders guiding the business were in stark contrast.

Another example of the power and relevance of belief in business is branding. This concept has extended from magazine ads and media commercials for our favorite products and services into *personal* branding—the idea that you and what you represent can be considered your personal brand. Brands are made possible through the belief(s) they instill in others. Whether low-grade or premium, the thoughts they invite consistently and repeatedly create the threads in the fabric of belief in the brand.

The greatest brands often evoke the same two or three thoughts from hundreds of thousands of consumers simply at the mention of their name or the sight of their logo. And, if done well, these two or three thoughts are consistent with what they want their brand to represent. This is intentional. They want us to keep thinking about their product or service in terms of our experience, witnessed behavior, and communication with it.

What thoughts come to mind at the mention of Starbucks? Coca-Cola? Amazon? Google? Apple? Microsoft? If I were to list the response of 100 readers for each of those brands, I would bet big there would be a consistency in response. That's the power of fully embracing the relevance of belief in business.

Last, and most relevant in the context of leading change, in order to motivate and inspire an organization effectively toward a change vision, there is a need for a guiding belief or belief system. For example, when embarking upon an organizational restructure, the belief system encompasses the reasons that the change will serve the business for the better:

- We will enjoy improved cross-functional collaboration.

- We will enable for the first time direct-to-customer relations-building for our technical leadership.

- Brand-unique customer and market needs will be seamlessly integrated into our innovation portfolios.

When these type of "beliefs to better" are shared and consistently supported by elements at the base of the change delta (communication, leadership behavior, and employee experience), they become anchors for the hearts and minds who are actually executing the vision.

What follows is a belief *system* that, when practiced, enables strengthened resilience, evolution to best self, and empowerment to grow through any change, transition, disruption, or transformation. This belief system is called Change Enthusiasm.

Chapter at a Glance

- Influencing belief is the key to influencing lasting change.

- Life experience, witnessed behavior, and communication (verbal, written, and perceived) serve to influence and reinforce thoughts.

- Belief is a thought you keep thinking.

- Belief manifests in business through brand equity building, company purpose and values, and "beliefs to better" integration toward successful change adoption.

- Change Enthusiasm is a belief system that, when practiced, strengthens individual resilience and empowers growth and fulfillment through change.

DEFINING OUR RELATIONSHIP WITH CHANGE

Before we dive into the practical application of the Change Enthusiasm mindset, let's define *when* to employ it. Throughout our careers, we experience change in many ways, whether it's through advancement, a lost job, a new manager, or pivoting into a new industry. Across my decade-plus tenure in corporate America and several years as an entrepreneur and business owner, I have discovered that the most common roles in relationship to change can be distilled to: creator, leader, and executor.

Change in business is necessary in order to remain competitive and relevant, although it can be challenging and tough at times. When we become responsible for change in our organization or professional life that we didn't ask for or take part in creating, it can be quite daunting. By establishing and understanding our role in a given *change situation* we become empowered to redefine change itself. We can give it a name. A personality. We can transform our view of change into a *thing* called Change. It becomes something tangible. Something with which we can develop a relationship. In doing so, the complexity associated with Change becomes more manageable.

Our most intimate relationships, when we are open and willing to learn, can become breeding grounds for personal growth. The film *Cast Away* became more interesting when the character Wilson, a volleyball, was introduced. When Tom Hanks's character developed a relationship with a volleyball, he established not only companionship but also the opportunity to express and learn about himself. As viewers, we were able to get closer to Tom Hanks's character through his interactions with Wilson. When we establish a relationship with Change something special happens. We create a dynamic in which we can learn about ourselves. What if you strived to establish, explore, and understand your relationship with Change?

To do this, imagine Change as an object. Keeping in the spirit of Wilson, let's imagine Change as a ball. Now imagine the dynamics involved with being successful in your business as the *relationship* you have with this ball. The ball gets introduced into your game, replacing the previous object used during play that you knew so well; now you must understand and build a different relationship. Some aspects from the prior relationship may still carry over, while others will not. A new ball and the new relationship dynamics involved therein can, at times, have the ability to create an entirely new game, making the prior game obsolete. This is true for any change in business: new process, industry disruption, lost job, new employee, new management, new operating tool, or new success metrics. Understanding and nurturing a healthy relationship with Change is a necessity in effectively navigating change.

Just as Tom Hanks's character in *Cast Away* became a friend, caregiver, and protector of Wilson during his deserted island journey, you could be the creator, leader, and/or executor of Change in the game of business. Let's walk through each and define the critical keys to ensuring the health and effectiveness of the relationship.

THE CHANGE CREATOR

The Change Creator gives birth to the possibility of Change from a spark emanating from within. In this role, Change comes crawling to you in the middle of the night ready to be nurtured. As alluded to in Chapter 2, Change in its infancy is simply an idea or thought energy. By crystallizing the idea into something that can be made manifest, you *create* the possibility for Change, such as a new workflow that drives out inefficiencies, an innovation that makes life better, a business that has the potential to disrupt an entire industry, or a mission statement that can influence and inspire thousands.

The Change Creator's Keys to a Healthy Relationship with Change

- **Ideation:** Allowing an idea for change to greet your thoughts

- **Discovery:** Finding and defining a change vision that is going to make your reality better

- **Experimentation:** Fine-tuning and developing a change vision through a process of trial and error to ensure it best aligns with your intention

- **Reflection:** Imagining a reality that includes the change and how that reality may be impacted

- **Dedication:** Developing and nurturing the change idea through focused effort and attention

- **Communication:** Influencing others through words and language to align to the change vision

When I was a middle manager leading innovation delivery on a multibillion-dollar brand, I had an idea to restructure my organization to maximize efficiency and drive out losses. I had been in my role long enough to understand where the majority of the losses stemmed from and discovered opportunities to improve. In that particular company there were human resources tools available to assess organizational effectiveness. Once I had a clear idea, I began leveraging these tools to redefine the structure of my teams, including responsibilities of my and adjacent divisions. After several weeks of reflection and multiple iterations, I landed on something I presented to the senior leadership of all organizations impacted by the potential change. I had become a Change Creator, creating the *possibility* for big change across organizations.

THE CHANGE LEADER

As a Change Leader you have been tasked to lead others through Change. You are responsible for designing the plays with Change integrated in a way that will ensure wins. This requires understanding how the Change might impact the game play and the players themselves. You must coach the team on the dimensions of the Change and through execution of your plays.

The Change Leader's Keys to a Healthy Relationship with Change

- **Relationship building:** Working effectively and efficiently with others to bring change into reality

- **Comprehension:** Understanding the factors, dimensions, and critical areas of the change; understanding what's working and what's not working during change implementation and making the necessary adjustments to optimize

- **Communication:** Influencing others toward the change vision with words and language, guiding the implementation of the change into reality

- **Compliance:** Adhering to the guidelines, instructions, and/or directions of change

- **Dedication:** Teaching and implementing the change with focused effort and attention

- **Flexibility:** Achieving the most effective and efficient implementation through a willingness to adapt to change

- **Support:** Providing direction, action, and/or information to those implementing the change to enable success

Once I had my organizational redesign idea aligned with senior leadership—including my vision of how it would be implemented—it was time to lead the change. I had to find the right rollout strategy. How would I present the change to the team? How quickly would they need to begin any new responsibilities? How quickly would those employees who would be new to my division need to be in place? How much would I need to rely on senior leadership to help roll out the changes, given the fact that multiple organizations would be impacted? As the Change Leader, I needed to answer these questions in order to have clarity of communication with everyone who would be impacted.

THE CHANGE EXECUTOR

As a Change Executor, you have been handed Change with the expectation that you will make it happen. You have to figure out how to win the game with this new Change. It feels different. It handles differently. It takes different muscles to throw it. The way in which you had been working and the associated level of comfort with getting your work done has been turned on its head. You have to understand your relationship with Change quickly and efficiently to continue delivering what you're responsible for and keep the business running smoothly.

The Change Executor's Keys to a Healthy Relationship with Change

- **Dedication:** Implementing the change with focused effort and attention

- **Comprehension:** Understanding the vision, factors, dimensions, and critical areas of change; requires asking the right questions to ensure this understanding

- **Communication:** Influencing others with words and language to convey what's working and what's not working during change implementation

- **Effort:** Taking action to implement and optimize the change throughout the change journey

- **Flexibility:** Adapting as necessary through the change implementation to maximize effectiveness and efficiency

- **Compliance:** Adhering to the guidelines, instructions, and/or directions of the Change Leader

Once my organizational restructure was approved by senior leadership, my team and those employees impacted by the new structure had to implement the change vision. There was learning along the way, and as a result, the original structure was fine-tuned and modified to reach the best possible outcome.

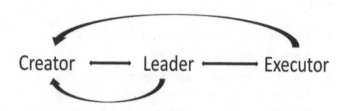

These roles and relationships are not mutually exclusive. You can embody all three for any given Change. Making Change happen is not a linear process. Creators have to lead. Leaders have to execute. Executors and leaders alike have the power to influence creation by providing feedback on what's working and what's not. Given these dynamics, the parameters of every relationship are critical to promote the efficiency and effectiveness of achieving the intended Change.

The mindset of Change Enthusiasm can be employed across all three roles to enable a healthier, more fulfilling, and effective relationship with Change.

Chapter at a Glance

- Defining your relationship with Change is critical to ensure growth.

- There are three core roles possible in Change:
  - The Change Creator
  - The Change Leader
  - The Change Executor

- The Change Creator gives the idea that makes Change possible.

- The Change Leader guides individuals, teams, or the organization as a whole through the implementation of Change.

- The Change Executor brings the Change into reality.

- These relationships with Change are not mutually exclusive. It is possible to engage in more than one relationship for a given Change.

PART II

THE PRACTICAL APPLICATION

THE SIGNAL

Imagine you're a midlevel executive at a large company. You have 30 people who report to you and your organization has been exceeding expectations for the past couple of years, leading breakthrough growth for your sector. You have an excellent working relationship with your manager. It's arguably one of the best you've ever experienced. She is supportive, collaborative, exceptionally bright, challenging, and filled with integrity. You walk into the office on a Tuesday morning feeling refreshed after a solid eight hours of sleep and ready to tackle the day. Shortly after you dock your laptop and log in, your manager pings you on the company's instant messaging platform. She wants you to stop by her office for a moment. It's rare that this happens but when it does it usually means she has important news impacting you and/or your organization.

On the short walk down you're mentally running down the list of what she possibly could have to share. Was it good news? Had bonuses come early? Certainly, it wasn't bad news. You know you've been kicking tail in the results department over the past several months, including the presentation you gave to the executive team just last week. Your mental gears begin shifting back to that particular review, and with every step toward your manager's office your confidence is boosted. You recall how you were able to shine in spite of Mark B, your manager's peer (who leads a different department), being in the room. Mark B always had something negative or unproductive to say, and you could never understand how he had gotten so high up in the organization given his attitude and ineptitude. He was that type of senior leader you had to tolerate but ultimately avoided whenever possible. But because of your preparation and the stellar work of your team you had a near-perfect response to his every comment and question.

You pull yourself from your thoughts as you reach your manager's office, give a quick hello to her executive assistant, and walk in feeling confident and content. As you're getting seated she joins you at the table and proceeds to share some news: She has been promoted and there will be a few organizational shifts as a result. One of these impacts is you. Effective the following week, you and your organization will be reporting to Mark B.

Have you undergone anything similar in your professional career? Have you been given a new manager you've struggled to gel with in the past or possibly never respected? Have you been told you would be taking on new responsibilities without any additional resources to help manage them? Have you ever experienced the biggest deal since starting your business and full-time entrepreneurial pursuits falling through in the 11th hour? These are the changes that disrupt. These are the changes that show up on our path like brick walls appearing out of thin air, leading us to run smack into them face first in full stride. These changes hurt. They are painful and often inspire the signal emotions of change: fear, anxiety, frustration, grief, and anger.

We've all experienced these types of changes and the emotions that follow. The question is, what did we DO in those moments? When those signal emotions shook our entire body or left our mouths dry and minds numb. What do *you* do? Recognizing the presence of the emotion and then stepping outside of it so as not to allow it to cloud our judgment and subsequent actions is much easier said than done. This is especially true in a business context. Your reputation is on the line, and, more important: your paycheck. After hearing upsetting news, you can't yell at your manager or throw a chair across the room without consequences. And those consequences won't just impact you, they will impact your family.

We play it cool in front of managers, peers, and direct reports while ignoring or suppressing the ocean of emotion within. Then after those grueling eight or nine hours at work, we pull the release valve and vent the emotion out to anyone and everyone who will listen. This relief feels great over cocktails or a long phone conversation on the couch. That is until we tighten the valve up again when we walk into the office the following day, effectively turning our "work self" on again.

Though this may seem to be the easier choice, by hiding the emotions you experience at work, you are missing out on being the best you that you can possibly be each and every day. You are suppressing a part of yourself as you strive to attain that evasive work-life balance. This concept sets up an internal struggle to balance a work self and a *true* self. But what if instead we strived to **integrate** work into a full and enriched life? What if instead of suppressing or hiding emotion in our work we allowed that energy to exist, using it to guide and inform our decision-making?

Emotion is not only inevitable but a necessity in any successful business. Emotion accelerates a company mission. Emotion is the undercurrent of culture. Emotion is a powerful energetic entity that when understood, embraced, and effectively harnessed fuels authentic success and competitive advantage. An emotionally self-aware leader has the ability to inspire thousands.

The first step of Change Enthusiasm is discovering how you experience the signal emotions of change and how they manifest within your body, stepping outside the emotions to view them objectively and explore the meaning behind them.

DISCOVERING HOW SIGNAL EMOTIONS MANIFEST WITHIN <u>YOU</u>

*A man that does not know how to be angry
does not know how to be good.*

— Henry Ward Beecher

Do you know how anger or frustration shows up within you? Do you know what anxiety actually *feels* like? If asked, could you describe it in vivid detail? Could you describe the specific physiological responses that occur in your body? Does your hair rise? Do you experience dry mouth? Does your heartbeat quicken? Could you describe your behavior toward others when you're experiencing anger? Do you shut down and keep others out? Do you yell in exasperation to get your point across? What do you do when you feel your signal emotions?

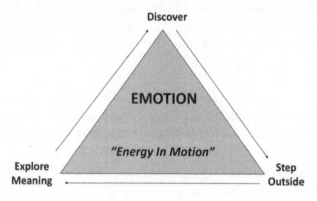

Figure 4: The practice of the first step of Change Enthusiasm can be broken down into three parts: Discover, Step Outside, and Explore Meaning.

Knowing the answers to these questions is the initial part of practicing the first step of Change Enthusiasm: embracing our emotional energy as signals to our greatest growth opportunities. It is not until we are able to recognize and acknowledge the presence of these emotions that we can embrace them as the gifts they are. In Figure 4, the process behind the first step of Change Enthusiasm is depicted:

- Discover
- Step outside
- Explore meaning

In the remainder of this chapter we'll walk through this process and review exercises to help you put it into daily practice.

Let's begin at the top of the pyramid: discover. This is about discovering how your signal emotional energy manifests within. It's about recognizing and acknowledging the existence of those emotions. Right now, do a gut check. Ask yourself: Am I able to recognize and acknowledge the signal emotions of change on a consistent basis? If there is even the faintest hint of doubt in your ability to do so, great. You can now trust that you're reading these pages for a reason.

I had the honor of asking American high jump record holder Chaunté Lowe if she can recognize her signal emotions on a consistent basis and I have to admit, I was surprised by her response. Chaunté and I met at Georgia Tech where we were both on the school's very first women's indoor NCAA track and field championship team. Chaunté has a boundless joy and exuberance for life. It wasn't uncommon for her to be dancing between sets in the weight room or laughing uncontrollably during warm-up on the track. She is simply a pleasure to be around. She has an effervescence that draws people to her.

Chaunté grew up in meager surroundings with a single mother and a father in prison most of her life. She and her siblings experienced homelessness when she was in the sixth grade, but by then she had already made a life-altering decision. At age four she decided she was going to be an Olympian and nothing was going to stand in the way of that, including being without a home. She was a standout talent specializing in the high jump, which eventually landed her a scholarship to Georgia Tech.

During her freshman year, Chaunté fell in love. It was an unhealthy relationship, but she was determined to make it work. The relationship reached its tipping point when her boyfriend took her hard-earned airline travel buddy passes and went to Hawaii *without her.* It might sound silly reading that, but for 19-year-old Chaunté it was devastating. She sunk into a deep depression. After she ingested a potentially fatal dose of pills, she was found and saved by a teammate.

It was after nearly taking her own life that she made a promise to herself that she would never again allow anger and hatred to fuel her. This was her greatest lesson: Do not let anger define the rest of your life.

Because of that experience Chaunté can describe in vivid detail how anger, frustration, and anxiety show up within her. Because of that knowing, Chaunté is skilled in quickly recognizing this emotional energy and transforming it into fuel for her growth. When I asked what she does when she gets her signal emotions, to quote her directly, she said, "I fix it, damnit!" This is a skill she's relied on heavily throughout her career. But before we delve deeper into Chaunté's journey and the remaining two parts of the process depicted in Figure 4, let's do an exercise to improve your skill of discovering your emotional energy.

Exercise: Understanding Your Emotional Energy

Materials Required:

1. A willingness to be honest and nonjudgmental with yourself

2. A pen or pencil

Directions: Think of the most recent time you've experienced the signal emotions of change and fill out the chart below. Please avoid as best as you can any desire to judge yourself. This exercise simply serves to better understand how these emotions manifest through *you*. There are no right or wrong responses. The more honest you can be with yourself, the greater the value you'll receive.

Signal Emotion	Experience Description	Physiological Responses	Behavioral Responses
ANGER			
FRUSTRATION			
GRIEF			
ANXIETY			
FEAR			

STEPPING OUTSIDE EMOTION

The second part of this step in Change Enthusiasm is probably the most difficult: stepping outside of our emotion. By becoming aware of the conscious thoughts that bring attention to a given emotion and *changing* them, we circumvent *becoming* that emotion or continuing to nurture the thoughts that inspire negative emotional energy. This is one of the most challenging parts of being human!

When facing the disappointment, devastation, loss, or tragedy that change and disruption can bring, emotion often overwhelms us. Those signal emotions can cause us to experience a seemingly uncontrollable urge to create thoughts and build narratives that draw greater and greater attention to that negative energy—just as Chaunté did so many years ago in her dorm room when she was enraged by the actions of her boyfriend. Her thoughts took her deep into a downward spiral, pulling her attention into the flame of anger and hatred all the way to the thought of ending her life. Chaunté's is an extreme example, but there is certainly danger in falling into a downward mental spiral. Whether it manifests as stalled career growth, binge eating or drinking, abusive relationships, or a suicide attempt. But there's good news. You have the power to step outside of those emotions and view them objectively as the gifts they are. No matter how strong the feeling, trust that you have the ability to step outside of it, recognize the conscious thoughts surrounding that emotion, and change the thoughts to transform that emotion.

"I FIX IT, DAMNIT!"

Chaunté's childhood dream came true at age 20 when she made her very first U.S. Olympic team in 2004. With her tenacity, ability, and passion, she went on to compete in the next three Olympic Games and six World Championships. She won the gold at the 2012 World Championships in Istanbul, Turkey. Her career took her all over the globe, from Morocco to Russia to Brazil to China, where she competed against other elite athletes. During this time, Chaunté married and had three beautiful children with her husband, Mario Lowe.

Chaunté was to participate in her fifth Olympic Games in Tokyo, but the 2020 Summer Olympics were postponed due to the coronavirus pandemic. She had been monitoring a lump in her breast for months and finally decided to share the information with her doctors. It turned out to be cancer.

This highly resilient, world-class athlete and mother of three immediately felt the signal emotions of disruption coursing through her body. She was upset. She was angry. She cried. She asked herself, How could this have happened to me? She found herself venturing into that dark place once more, mad at the world. That same place where she had nearly lost her life so many years ago. Recognizing the walls were closing in, she became aware of the conscious thoughts that were inspiring that ocean of emotion and accompanying mental darkness, thoughts like *I'm going to die.* She decided to change those thoughts. She did this by asking herself, What can I do to fix it? Once that question was posed something within her answered that a solution existed. With that belief growing moment by moment, she flipped a mental switch into the lane of What *will* I do to fix it? and in doing so transitioned from a mental state of helplessness to empowerment.

In those initial dark moments, when Chaunté allowed herself to succumb to the negative emotional energy, she felt helpless. She existed as a victim of her diagnosis. She existed as a product of her circumstance. By *believing* there was a solution to the problem and allowing her actions to be guided accordingly, she freed herself to actively work toward changing the outcome she feared most: death.

She read thousands of reviews in search of the best oncologists and surgeons. Ultimately she settled on a course of action that she believed would give her the greatest chance for the outcome she most desired: life. By the time we sat down together in June 2020, she was healthy, cancer-free, training, working on a book of her own, and just as effervescent as ever.

Chaunté's ability to step outside of her dark moment reinforces that through the power of belief, it's possible to create the freedom and space we need to take control of our situation and work toward our desired outcome. You may be asking yourself, How? How can I, in my darkest moments, overwhelmed by the rage, frustration, or anxiety that change and disruption brings . . . how can I find the light of belief within?

The next exercise will help you do just that. It is inspired by Chaunté and what she did to keep herself from sinking back into that dark place throughout her cancer journey. After her mastectomy and prior to her first round of chemotherapy, she decided to create a video *of* herself *for* herself. She strove to capture the energy that fuels her best: joy. With all the exuberance she could muster, she became her own cheerleader by sharing her joy with her future self, who she imagined would be struggling, sick, and overwhelmed by all of her signal emotions. In this video, Chaunté nurtured her belief that she would get through it. She reinforced her strength. She reminded herself of all the things in her life that brought her joy each and every day. She reminded herself of those parts of life that are worth the fight.

In this, Chaunté teaches an important lesson: Whenever times are challenging you must maintain a reserve of whatever energizes you. She says that when you're going through a transition or major change, you have to have a bag of tricks to get yourself out of the negative thoughts that bring attention to negative feelings. And it's important to delve into that bag once you've recognized and acknowledged those signal emotions. For her, that video was an effective trick. She watched it whenever she had tough days and it consistently helped to inspire better feelings. It consistently helped to keep her out of the downward spiral of depression.

I believe Chaunté got this one right. Who better to change your conscious thought to inspire a better feeling than YOU? Complete the exercise below as a gift to *your* future self for when you may be overwhelmed with the signal emotions of change.

Exercise: A Gift to Your Future Self

Materials Required:

1. A video recording device, e.g., your smartphone

2. A pen or pencil

Directions: Answer the questions below, then create a video addressed to your future self. A sample script is provided, but feel free to create your own message. The intent is to shake your future self out of the grasp of your signal emotions and into a conscious space where you can view these emotions objectively and get about the business of evolving to better. If you're not in the mind space to create the video now, feel free to revisit this exercise at a later date.

1. Describe a time when you've overcome a significant and stressful change challenge. State the challenge and how you overcame it.

   _____

   _____

   _____

2. Share one reason you're better because you saw your way through the challenge described in the previous entry.

   _____

   _____

   _____

3. What do you feel are your top three qualities?

   _____

   _____

   _____

4. What are you consistently told are the top two strengths you bring to your work (e.g., fresh perspective, high energy, creative solutions, comic relief, impeccable writing)?

   _____

   _____

   _____

5. What are you doing when you feel you are at your best (e.g., helping others, cooking, singing, presenting on a topic in which you have a depth of knowledge)?

   _____

   _____

   _____

6. What brings you joy?

   _____

   _____

   _____

Sample Video Script:

Hey rock star! First off, know that I love you and you're amazing. You're having a tough go of it right now. And that's okay. I've been there. You know I've been there because you were there with me. Remember when we had to ***insert response to #1***. If it weren't for that insanely stressful time we never would have* *insert response to #2*. You know what that tells me? No matter how dark, sucky, or desperate things may feel right now . . . there's opportunity in this. And I know you're going to find it and maximize it! You've done it before, and you will do it again.

Because you are *insert response to #3*. And you are consistently appreciated for bringing *insert response to #4*. If you need to sit in these emotions for a couple of days, so be it. I'm cool with that as long as you can make me a promise. After sitting in acknowledgment of these emotions, promise you'll do what I know you're capable of doing: Explore how to transform this emotional energy to fuel your growth, to fuel your evolution through this beautiful thing called life. To fuel you into doing more *insert response to #5*. To continue enjoying your *insert response to #6*. Yeah, remember: Although you're in a challenging spot right now, life is good. Life is really good. Trust that I'm here with you carrying tremendous belief in you. Belief that you'll see your way through this. I know it. You've got this. You've got this.

EXPLORING EMOTIONAL MEANING

Referring back to Figure 4, once you've acknowledged a signal emotion and consciously stepped outside of it, the final part of the process is exploring its meaning and naming those thoughts that are seeking to pull your attention into them. This final part is the essence of *emotional self-awareness*, a subskill of emotional intelligence.

If you're like me, you've had an emotion hit and then had it followed by an avalanche of thoughts that made that particular emotion more and more apparent. Let's take the example of my hearing the news of the Duracell acquisition. With a perceived loss of a company and culture I loved, my immediate feelings were grief and anxiety. Those feelings, or signal emotions, generated the following thoughts:

This business is being acquired by a company I don't know.
My dream of retiring with P&G isn't going to happen.
Gosh, why did I even transfer into this business?
Why didn't I see this coming? What the hell am I going to do?
New management won't know me.
I'm losing my support system.
I'm losing my close connection with friends and colleagues.
I no longer have job security.

I'll probably get a new manager. What if I don't get on well with him or her?

I may not survive the acquisition. I may be without a job very soon.

I'll soon be back on the market looking for a job . . . and it's tough out there right now.

I won't be able to pay my mortgage.

I'll have to sell my house and move back in with my parents.

Just like that, moments after hearing my business was being acquired, in my mind I was grief-stricken, anxious, jobless, and living on my parents' couch. It sounds comical, but that's how quickly our thoughts can propel us into downward spirals. Have you had a similar experience? Have you allowed your thoughts to spiral down to where the light gets turned off and the darkness persists? Thought carries us there and negative emotional energy shuts the light out. The negative emotional energy is the cloud of darkness surrounding us.

Once we can view our conscious thought separately from that cloud through practicing the exercises in this chapter, we are able to explore the cloud, including the emotion and associated thoughts it houses. We take our rightful place in the driver's seat of our change experience, becoming empowered to assess the landscape and the power of that emotional energy with unclouded judgment, no pun intended. (Well, maybe it was intended a little.)

No one believes that the thoughts that pull our attention into negative emotional energy can be stopped in their tracks and removed from our consciousness more than Chaunté Lowe. Chaunté says these thoughts must be pulled like weeds from a garden. Without their removal, you'll be unable to move toward your better self. Without their removal, you'll remain suspended in that dark place, held securely by those thoughts you allow to take root.

Though Chaunté experienced hearing perhaps the worst news an assumingly healthy person could receive and walked the challenging road that followed, her breast cancer diagnosis and journey back to full health was not the toughest obstacle she's ever faced in her professional year. When asked of the toughest, the disruption wrought with the strongest signal emotions she's ever experienced, Chaunté reflected and then regaled me with her "defining moment in 2008."

Chaunté made her second Olympic team in 2008. In that very same year, she completed her college education and had her first child. Simply finishing her degree and training for the games would have been challenging enough. Chaunté had taken fewer and fewer credits from semester to semester after signing a contract with Nike in 2005; eventually she took a full year break to travel the world competing. Determined to attain her degree, she had to lobby the president of Georgia Tech directly to be granted allowance to take 49 credits in one school year, more than the allowed number at that time. Her request was granted and soon after the start of that hefty school year and training for the games, she discovered she was pregnant. She told me it was the most challenging 12 months she's ever experienced. Not only was there challenge in the sheer academic and athletic workload but also in needing to be successful in those endeavors while experiencing life growing inside of her.

There were more people in her inner circle than she can remember who advised her to get an abortion. There were those who compassionately warned that having a child at that time would inevitably mean the death of her professional athletic career. Thwarting that advice, she made the decision to have the baby. Soon following that decision, the next theme she heard from those around her was that she wouldn't or *couldn't* come back and compete at the same level.

Her own signal emotions and the words she heard around her invited Chaunté back into those thoughts that were ready to carry her into a downward spiral:

I'm shooting my professional career in the foot.

Having a baby means I'm resigning from the highest athletic stage.

I'm giving up on my lifelong dreams.

But as quickly as those thoughts presented themselves, Chaunté stopped them in their tracks. She explored their meaning, determined they were fundamentally misaligned with her own beliefs, and then pulled them from her consciousness like weeds.

Chaunté made it through that year, giving birth to a healthy baby girl, and though she originally finished sixth on the 2008 Olympic stage, she later advanced to third after three competitors were disqualified. In 2010 she broke the American high jump record three times, proving that she was back, not only able to compete at the highest level but to DEFINE the highest level. This part of Chaunté's story exemplifies how exploring our negative emotional energy and supporting thoughts can help pivot the way we experience tough and challenging change.

One final point regarding Chaunté's thought/weed analogy before we progress into practicing this concept. I just loved this analogy and it inspired me to do a bit of digging (yes, that pun was definitely intended) into the science of weeds. What I found was fascinating. We often hear about the importance of pursuing our life's purpose. Find your purpose, that thing you love, and you'll never work a day in your life. You've heard it, right? Well, weeds have their life's purpose figured out in spades: growth. Weeds exist to grow and multiply and they pursue their purpose unabashedly every single day. And even though when weeds are allowed to live this purpose they pose a detriment to the health of a crop or garden, mitigated weed growth can prove very beneficial.

Weeds inform us of soil type. When we can understand the type of weeds growing in a garden, we can better understand the type of nutrients present and/or lacking in that soil and why a crop may or may not be thriving. Weeds also build our soil. Because they grow fast, they produce carbon quickly. When the weeds die, this carbon remains present in the soil, helping it to build structure and retain water.

Thought/Weed Analogy Explored		
Thoughts that Nurture Negative Emotions	=	Weeds
Mental State	=	Soil
How We Wish to Experience the Change	=	Intended Crop

Figure 5: A thought versus weed analogy defined.

Exploring the analogy in Figure 5, if we consider the thoughts that nurture the intensity of negative emotion as weeds, our mental state as soil, and how we feel during our experience or circumstance as an intended crop, how might these thoughts be serving us in some way? Just as analyzing weeds can inform soil type and what nutrients are present or deficient to grow an intended crop, analyzing your thoughts can inform you of your mental state and what's present or lacking to reach the desired experience of your circumstance. When Chaunté pulled her negative thoughts up like weeds, following this analogy, she could have analyzed them to become even better informed of how best to improve her mental state. When you analyze negative thoughts once they're "pulled," you learn what changes should be made in your mental state to create a desired feeling or experience.

Just as weeds can build the soil through carbon deposits once they die, thoughts can build your understanding of how you respond to signal emotions. As this understanding grows, you become better prepared for the next challenge. You experience personal growth and a strengthened resiliency. The takeaway being not to ignore or judge yourself for having these thoughts but rather understand and embrace their value. Let's walk through an exercise to put this into practice.

Exercise: Taking an Emotional Inventory

Materials Required:

1. Self-compassion

2. A pen or pencil

Directions: Think of a current change challenge you're facing. Reflect on any signal emotions you have experienced around this situation in the past few weeks and complete the chart below.

Signal Emotion	What Inspired This Emotion?	What Thoughts Are Associated?
ANGER		
FRUSTRATION		
GRIEF		
ANXIETY		
FEAR		

Putting It into Practice: A Frustrated Executive on the Verge of Quitting

Shayla's Story

I am an account executive for a large business solutions company in charge of owning and growing my portion of the business. In this role, I cold-call potential clients to establish and build relationships and I maintain strong relationships with current customers. I have been in this role for about nine months now. I started two weeks before the shutdown for COVID-19. I wasn't even complete with my training before we moved everything to a virtual environment and began working from home.

Though I know I am not the only one who struggles with mental illness in their personal or professional life, I have struggled with anxiety my entire adult life and I have had to come up with ways to change the way I view certain situations. I knew taking on a new and unfamiliar job was a risk. I worked at a country club for seven years prior to this role. I remained there because it was a position I was familiar with and I was good at it.

This job was new to me and a HUGE change. A change that hit me hard. I almost quit after being there just three months despite being in the middle of a pandemic. People were getting laid off left and right, and I almost quit because I was frustrated with how I wasn't able to jump into this new job full steam ahead. I was waking up every day with a gut feeling that I was failing in an industry known for "weeding out the weak." It was not a healthy mindset.

Being new to the industry, there were many things that were unfamiliar and uncomfortable to me: the way that others treated me, comments made by my superiors, and the complexity of the processes. Asking for help was like pulling teeth, bringing more frustration and anger. Then I learned about the strategy of Change Enthusiasm. In this strategy, I found a new way of viewing things. My frustration and anxiety were signals. Viewing these emotions as invitations to growth, I began to tell myself that my business was run by *me*. If I wanted to succeed, I needed to get excited about my opportunity to learn and grow. Moving into the second step of Change Enthusiasm, I explored my opportunity. I slowly began to break down the barriers of being anxious about speaking up around my co-workers and bosses. In practicing the final step of Change Enthusiasm, I chose to speak up. I chose to actively engage in improving *my* business. And those choices really paid off! I'm on my way to being in the president's club, an elite group of account executives, and I am earning the respect of so many people both in the office and with my client base. I'm so grateful I put Change Enthusiasm into practice, accepting my anxiety's invitation into my opportunity to grow, and above all . . . not quitting.

EMOTIONAL CONTAGION: THE POWER OF YOUR ENERGETIC INFLUENCE

Have you ever walked into a meeting and felt the tension in the room even before anyone spoke? The kind of tension you could figuratively cut with a knife? The type of feeling that causes you to second-guess nearly every thought before speaking it aloud? The type of feeling that can create a deafening silence because no one wants to take the perceived risk of speaking up? The type of feeling you can't wait to escape and talk about with co-workers in the break room? Or have you ever met someone and immediately felt lighter and happier? That person you would describe as having *infectious, boundlessly joyful* energy? The person you find yourself excited to see outside of work? The person you feel proud and fortunate to have as part of your team? That person everyone wants at their meetings because you always just feel better when they're around?

Well, these effects, these feelings are made possible by a very interesting and well-studied phenomenon called emotional contagion, which means our emotions have the ability to be "caught" by those around us. Researchers of psychology believe that it is best conceptualized as a compounding family of psychophysiological behavior and social phenomena. In essence, emotional contagion is a phenomenon wherein an emotion that arises from one individual is acted upon by one or more other individuals, yielding corresponding and complementary emotions in these individuals (Elaine Hatfield 1997).[2]

It's the reason we may feel down after trying to cheer up someone who is upset. It's the reason we feel good after having coffee with someone who is highly self-confident and joyful. Honestly, it's the reason that speakers like myself can make a living standing on a stage or in front of a webcam just talking. The energy that we radiate through our words, facial expressions, and body language is *caught* by our audience members, making them feel just as charged and energized as we are.

Understanding emotional contagion helps us to be aware that our emotional energy not only impacts us, but also those around us. Therefore, we must take responsibility for the energy we're putting out. As a leader, as a peer, as a

---

2.   Elaine Hatfield, John T. Cacioppo, Richard L. Rapson, *Emotional Contagion: Studies in Emotion and Social Interaction* (Cambridge CB2 1RP, England: Cambridge University Press, 1994).

manager, you put out energy that has the ability to strongly influence your direct reports, teams, and organizations—perhaps even more so than your words. This does not mean we should suppress our negative emotions. Remember, all emotion, whether perceived as negative or positive, is a gift that is meant to serve us. The risk of suppressing perceived negative emotions is far greater than allowing them to exist and be "caught" by those around us. What this concept can do is motivate us to accept the invitation into the opportunity our emotions present, then make a conscious effort to maximize that opportunity to grow.

Chapter at a Glance

- Emotion is not only inevitable but a necessity in any successful business.

- Emotion is a powerful energetic entity that when understood, embraced, and effectively harnessed fuels authentic success and competitive advantage.

- The first step of Change Enthusiasm is embracing the signal emotions of change as invitations to learn and grow. It is practiced through three actions:
  - Discovering the signal emotion
  - Stepping outside the emotion to view it objectively
  - Exploring the meaning of the emotion

- By understanding your emotional energy and how it may manifest within, you become better prepared to discover the presence of the signal emotions of change.

- Negative thoughts, once identified, can be pulled from our consciousness like weeds.

- Just as weeds can be analyzed to inform you of soil type and composition, negative thoughts related to change can be analyzed to inform you of how you handle these types of changes and how your thoughts could change to create a better experience.

- Taking an emotional inventory during a given change challenge will help you identify the emotions present as well as the thoughts inspiring those emotions.

- Emotional contagion is a phenomenon where an emotion expressed by one individual can be "caught" by another. This phenomenon is the reason we can sometimes feel inspired and happy when around one person, or tense and uneasy when around another.

- Our emotional energy impacts not only us but those around us.

THE OPPORTUNITY

When the storm is darkest it can be difficult to remember that the light still exists. You may have picked up this book because you're in your own storm, feeling the metaphorical wind and rain beating down upon you. Unable to see any ray of light through the clouds. Trust that you are not alone and allow for the *possibility* of opportunity to be present in every gust of wind, every drop of rain. Trust in the signal emotions of change to indicate the existence of opportunity, and then explore ways to capitalize on that opportunity. That is the second step of Change Enthusiasm.

FINDING A SEED OF TRUST

In the middle of difficulty lies opportunity.

— ALBERT EINSTEIN

In the wee hours of the morning of November 18, 1999, on the campus of Texas A&M, a 59-foot-high stack consisting of approximately 5,000 logs was being constructed for the school's long-held tradition: the Aggie bonfire. The Aggie bonfire tradition has come to represent the strong spirit of

Texas A&M's students, alumni, and supporters, as well as the "burning desire" to beat their top rival the University of Texas at Austin.

That morning, the massive structure was under construction when the unexpected happened. Logs began to shift until, like an avalanche, the entire structure tumbled to the ground, killing 12 students and injuring 27 more. It would be one of the most devasting events in the school's history.

One of the student leaders responsible for coordinating funerals and supporting students as they mourned through the storm was Elizabeth Gore. Given the magnitude of the disaster, the school's top-level administrators requested the support of top representatives of the state, including the governor and congressional leaders. In the face of tragedy, intense grief, overwhelm, and anger, Elizabeth learned how to lead through crisis by working alongside the best leaders Texas had to offer. She didn't know it, but this would serve her well in her future endeavors.

Elizabeth is now co-founder and president of Hello Alice, an online database focused on connecting and advancing women and minority small-business owners. With co-founder Carolyn Rodz and their team, Elizabeth is working to close the gap to the resources and funding required for business growth and success for marginalized populations versus their white male counterparts.

She is a firm believer that within crisis lies opportunity. In other words, within the context of Change Enthusiasm, Elizabeth would say that when the signal emotions of change are felt, they are calling your attention to the abundant opportunities surrounding you.

What comes to mind when you think of opportunity? How would you define it? You will see a few of my favorite opportunity-relevant quotes sprinkled throughout this chapter. It's probably one of the most quoted concepts in the world of motivational posters and self-help guidance. In case you're struggling to find the right words, how about we hand the ball to Merriam-Webster:

Opportunity (*noun*): (1) A favorable juncture of circumstances (2) a good chance for advancement or progress

A good *chance* for advancement or progress. As I mentioned in the start of this chapter, it's difficult to see or trust in a *chance for progress* when you're *in* the throes of change, paralyzed by your signal emotions. And because the language surrounding opportunity has become so cliché, you might find yourself jaded whenever someone offers it to you as you're drowning in your storm. During my time leading organizations at Procter & Gamble, whenever I was presented with more work, a challenging project, or asked to do something that no one else wanted to do, it was consistently framed as an "opportunity." Trust me, I've experienced that jaded feeling as well.

I can't tell you how many people I have connected with who are lost in their storms and blinded by the darkness. It is in these moments that the light must come from within, from a seed of trust, of *belief* in those signal emotions existing to invite you into opportunity. Seeing opportunity or your *chance for progress* is a matter of perspective built from experience and ultimately what grows from those seeds of belief.

You may be asking yourself: How do I find that seed? Actually, how do I even know it has been planted? Great question. Let's walk through an exercise to help you discover the answer.

Exercise: Finding Your Seed(s) of Trust

One of the tougher disruptions I've faced was losing two employees from my division in the middle of executing multiple high-priority business initiatives. These individuals chose to leave the company within weeks of one another. It was like one wave of tough news after the other. Combined they were responsible for more than a third of the work of my department. Their departure left a wake of action items that I and those who remained in the division had to quickly absorb. Not only did I have to redistribute the work, taking on a significant amount of it myself, but I also had to begin searching for the right people to backfill the now vacant positions.

I was overwhelmed. My days stretched longer and longer as I juggled all the work. I was unclear on how or even if my division was going to be able to keep everything on track. But we did. By using the tools and practices laid out in this book, in the short term we effectively absorbed the work, and in the long term we found replacements who quickly onboarded and excelled in their respective positions. This experience created a big seed of trust within me that no matter how dire the disruption appears, not only getting through it but *growing* through it is always possible.

This exercise serves to help you document your own seeds of trust—trust that you will not only be able to get through your toughest changes, but also that they offer you the greatest opportunity to become better and stronger.

Materials Required:

1. A willingness to explore tough times

2. A pen or pencil

Directions: Reflect on the deepest tragedy, disruption, or change challenge you've faced. This can be personal or professional. This can also be something you're experiencing right now. As you reflect, capture what has come true because of that challenge: connections, roles/positions, or a new perspective. Use the chart below as a guide. I've taken the liberty of populating it using my own example to get your gears turning.

Every response within columns two to four, if you allow them, will serve as seeds of trust that even in your toughest and most challenging change or disruption experience, there is something for your growth and betterment.

Change Event	New Connections	New Role(s)/ Position(s)	New Perspective
Briefly describe the change event.	*What new connection was made possible?*	*What professional role or position was made possible because I endured that event?*	*What is one new perspective gained?*
I lost two key employees while executing several high-priority business initiatives. The loss meant short-term absorption of their work by me and the rest of the division, and the urgent work of finding the right people to backfill the vacant positions.	The individuals hired to backfill the vacant positions were exceptional. They brought a fresh, vibrant energy to the entire department, doing work that excited and fulfilled them.	Given their effectiveness in absorbing the extra work, a couple of my employees' roles were slightly expanded, better positioning them for the next milestone in their career advancement.	When a team is cohesive, engaged, and working toward the same goal(s) they can deliver in unprecedented ways. Though the recruiting process can be optimized and streamlined to reduce the time line from job posting to job filling, it should not be rushed. Rushing recruitment into key positions has a high risk of bringing detriment in the long run, to both the company and the individual.

WHEN THE SEED OF TRUST GROWS, YOU GROW

Victory comes from finding opportunities in problems.

— Sun Tzu

Elizabeth Gore's seed of trust grew after the Aggie bonfire collapse of 1999, but it had been planted well before the logs came tumbling down. Raised by her parents and grandmother Opal, Elizabeth grew up on a cattle ranch. Her aspirations were to follow in the footsteps of her parents and manage the ranch. Growing up, she never really saw beyond the confines of the fences and posts of the ranch. That was, until she went to college.

She was the first female in her family to attend college. It was at Texas A&M that everything changed. Her eyes were opened to a new world and new experiences. During her early days at college, a friend got pregnant and had to drop out of school because there were still no childcare facilities or women's health-care facilities on campus. Texas A&M up until the '80s was an all-male military university. In the '90s there were no women-centric support systems on campus, which Elizabeth found both ridiculous and appalling. She decided to protest these circumstances that drove her friend to leave, eventually joining student government. She went on to work with the school's administration to build childcare and women's health facilities. That experience planted the seed of trust that from challenge comes opportunity. Elizabeth capitalized on the opportunity to create systemic change for the thousands of women who would follow her own tenure at the university. By pursuing this opportunity, she learned how energizing she found sitting at the intersection of what a community needed and seeing the creation and implementation of solutions to address those needs.

When the signal emotions of change stir us, I have found, as Elizabeth did, that one of the most immediate opportunities we are welcomed into is to learn more about ourselves. In fact, when asked to define opportunity, Elizabeth shared that she believes it to be "when someone gives you a chance or you find that chance yourself." She believes that once you've acknowledged that chance, whether you created it or it was handed to you, it's about milking that opportunity for everything it's worth. How do you learn? How do you expand?

It is in the face of change, disruption, transition, and transformation that we are enabled to learn the most about ourselves. Whether facing termination, filing bankruptcy, or dealing with a failed start-up, big change invites us *into a chance* to learn what lights us up inside and what doesn't. Change not only reminds us of our resiliency but invites us *into a chance* to grow it even stronger. Change invites us *into a chance* to determine what motivates us so that we can grow more in tune with ourselves, becoming better prepared for the next inevitable challenge. Let's bring this idea closer to home.

Exercise: Acknowledging Growth

Materials Required:

1. A willingness to get to know yourself
2. An open mind and heart
3. A pen or pencil

Directions: Reflect on the same challenge you used for the first exercise in this chapter. Consider what you learned about yourself through that challenge. Use the questions below as a guide.

- What made the challenge so difficult for me?

  _____

  _____

  _____

- What got me through that challenge (e.g., belief,
  person/relationship, activity)?

  _____

  _____

  _____

- What brought me joy during that time?

  _____

  _____

  _____

- How was I most changed as a result of that
  challenge?

  _____

  _____

  _____

- What did I discover no longer served me because
  of that challenge?

  _____

  _____

  _____

- What and/or whom do I appreciate more because of making it through that challenge?

_____

_____

_____

TRUST, THEN EXPLORE

Entrepreneurs are simply those who understand that there is little difference between obstacle and opportunity and are able to turn both to their advantage.

— Victor Kiam

Once the seed of trust has been planted and allowed to grow through the experience of change and disruption, we are able to explore the opportunity presented by those moments filled with signal emotions. But this is where things can become a bit muddled, as we often don't have full clarity about what exactly the opportunity is. Even when that seed of trust exists, as we assess the landscape of our situation, we may find that every corner, every inch may look just as bleak as the next.

Though she is now president and co-founder of a company generating millions in revenue, Elizabeth Gore's entrepreneurial journey has been far from easy. She has experienced several pivotal situations that required her to trust there was opportunity somewhere in the dimness. For me, having heard her story, three stand out.

The first happened midway through her collegiate career. The dimness came after making a big decision that she would not go back to the ranch and the family business after graduating, and the subsequent difficult conversation she had to have with her parents about that decision. Though she knew the ranch was not meant to be a part of her future, she didn't know what else was. She felt the slight tug of fear and anxiety having shut the door to a guaranteed career while not knowing what lay ahead. This is the same fear and anxiety that is often faced when a job is lost, or a business venture fails, or a new manager is given. When these signal emotions pop up, feasting on the unknown, they alert us into opportunity even when we can't see it. It's in the dimness that we must trust in the existence of that opportunity. This is exactly what Elizabeth had to do. She relied on a fire in her belly to experience all that life had to offer and trust that opportunity would present itself in the dimness of her unknown. And present itself it did.

Opportunity came knocking in a big way when Elizabeth landed a front-desk job for former president George H. W. Bush. He and his wife, proud residents of the state of Texas, were building his presidential library and school of government and public service at Texas A&M. The former president and first lady had an apartment on campus while these projects were under construction, which so happened to be in the same building as Elizabeth's desk. There she got to know Barbara and George Bush as people, not as political figures but as *human beings*. She was presented with an opportunity to fund-raise for the Bush school, and the Bushes paid for her master's degree in financial development, which she studied for at night while still working for them.

With great admiration for her work ethic and fondness for her friendship, the Bushes offered her *another* opportunity—to work in Washington, D.C., at their Points of Light Foundation following the completion of her master's degree. Founded in 1990 as a nonprofit organization to promote the spirit of volunteerism, Points of Light merged with the National Volunteer Center in 1991 and acted as a community hub to connect volunteers to opportunities, work with local nonprofits and businesses to establish and improve volunteer programs, and, overall, to bolster the local infrastructure for the volunteering community. The organization was about 500 volunteers deep by the time Elizabeth joined.

She sold her car to get enough money to go to D.C. to take the position. She was just a broke kid searching, learning, and evolving, but she loved every minute. Because she chose to trust that opportunity would present itself and to maximize each one that came across her path, Elizabeth found herself thriving and living her best life.

The second pivotal moment that required Elizabeth to trust in opportunity appeared during perhaps the darkest hour of the entire nation. On September 11, 2001, Elizabeth was working at the Points of Light Foundation in D.C. Just days after the attack, she and a few other colleagues at the foundation were flown to New York to lead the coordination of nonessential volunteer efforts at Ground Zero. It was a disruption experience that presented major opportunity. This time the opportunity was exponential personal growth. Through the pain and struggle, Elizabeth was invited to learn more about herself. With every signal emotion, like during the Aggie bonfire experience, she was invited into the opportunity to learn how to handle great tragedy—the kind that impacts the lives of thousands—with efficiency and grace.

When devastation hits in either our personal or professional worlds, the opportunity to learn about ourselves and how we navigate trying times is never greater. By remaining open to taking inventory of emotions, actions, and the result of these actions, we better prepare our futures selves to handle challenging change. We are invited into the opportunity to strengthen our resilience.

Elizabeth's resilience would continue to be relied upon and strengthened as she pursued her professional endeavors. She went on to spend several years in the Peace Corps, followed by nine years with the United Nations working predominantly in African refugee camps. Through these experiences she witnessed human resilience like none she had ever seen; they fed that seed of trust planted deeply within. And her career would continue to nurture her passion to build community and drive big change for women and underrepresented populations.

The third pivotal moment happened when Elizabeth was going for her first round of funding in support of her entrepreneurial endeavor, Hello Alice. By this time, she was a believer that no matter who you are, regardless of gender, race, ethnicity, or belief structure, that if you work your ass off, you're going to get there. Perhaps that belief was nurtured by the countless female refugees she witnessed come into a camp with next to nothing, holding small children, and within days had created commerce, figured out ways to get their hair fixed and clothing made, enabling them to show up in the outside world shining as brightly as the resilience lighting their internal world. But when Elizabeth and her co-founder, Carolyn Rodz, a Latina, went for their initial series investment round pitching to the big banks and venture capitalists it was, to pull a direct quote, "fucking hell."

They were told no 122 times in their first capital raise. When joined by their young, white male engineers who were part of the team, potential investors would greet them and *not* Elizabeth or her co-founder. Countless times Elizabeth and Carolyn were asked on dates and simply disrespected as the serious, intelligent, highly capable female business owners they are. During that funding round, they were both pregnant. Elizabeth said she can't count the number of times they were questioned by investors, "How are you going to do this with a baby?"

Elizabeth's signal emotions were ever-present, during and after every pitch, in the face of every single no she heard. Though she couldn't see it, these emotions were signaling her into opportunity, and like she had done so many times over the years prior, she trusted it was there.

Reliant upon that trust, Elizabeth and Carolyn eventually raised their first million dollars and got to work building the business. They had a significant amount of success from the start and quickly began expanding the platform, launching initiatives for the LGBTQ+ community and for entrepreneurs with disabilities. Excited by the success of these programs and in dire need of another capital injection, they were ready to pursue a second round of funding.

Certain the Series B funding experience would be different than before given their recent successes and Hello Alice's expansive growth in the market, Elizabeth jumped into pitch mode ready and determined. But the signal emotions of change quickly followed, as she and Carolyn were met with that same disrespect and rejection. Elizabeth was devastated. She was heartbroken. Her signal emotions were overwhelming, leaving her once again in that oh-so-familiar entrepreneurial darkness of not knowing what was next.

Our growth, in its evolutionary nature, almost demands intermittent periods of dimness—periods when we are unsure, rejected, devasted, and wrought with signal emotions. I believe it's from these periods that the greatest growth is possible. Elizabeth and her team eventually maximized the opportunity their Series B presented, successfully raising the capital, which catapulted them along a path of tremendous growth.

It's when we feel lost and unable to see any chance to progress that we must begin exploring what's possible, even if that exploration feels like walking in the dark while frantically searching for anything that feels like a light switch. This is the time when allowing our signal emotions to guide us can become effective at lighting the path of opportunity. When experiencing a big change, disruption, or transition, use the exercise below to put finding opportunity in change into practice.

Exercise: Allowing Signal Emotions to Light Your Path of Opportunity

Materials Required:

1. A list of close friends and/or mentors

2. An open mind

3. A pen or pencil

Directions: Use the chart below to explore options to transform any signal emotions and associated thoughts you may be experiencing at the moment. When we have embraced that opportunity exists within a given change challenge, this is the work needed to identify options that will maximize the opportunity.

Once completed, I have found it beneficial to share the chart with a close friend or mentor who has your best interest at heart. Listen to what perspective or guidance they offer regarding the options you have created and invite them to share new ones. Feel free to revisit the exercise in Chapter 4—"A Gift to Your Future Self"—as a refresher to those activities that bring you joy. Knowing these can inform your options to begin transforming your emotional energy.

Signal Emotion	What Thoughts Are Associated?	Productive Option(s) to Transform	Mentor Perspective
FEAR			
GRIEF			
ANXIETY			
ANGER			
FRUSTRATION			

Putting It into Practice:
A Team Called upon by a World in Crisis

I had the honor of engaging with a client who was a major player in the aviation industry while it was dealing with the fallout of the COVID-19 pandemic. As you might imagine, given the unthinkable reduction of air travel around the world their profits were significantly impacted, requiring constant negotiation and support from both federal and state government agencies to stay afloat. Despite the financial relief provided, major internal changes were critical to ensure long-term business health and sustainability. These changes included significant head count reductions. My firm was invited to engage with the company as part of an annual, year-end celebration event.

It was a celebration and recognition of the challenges and hardships overcome and the tireless efforts of every employee who made it possible. The timing of the event was just after the last wave of reductions were executed, so many were experiencing their signal emotions.

During the event, I met with a team that was being recognized for leading and executing efforts at an exceptional level throughout perhaps the most challenging year the company had ever faced. They truly embodied the mindset of Change Enthusiasm. In the midst of delivering their challenging internal goals and losing key resources, they were called upon by external public establishments to design and build a ventilator system to support a growing need. COVID-19 cases were climbing all over the world.

This team, who had historically led aircraft engine design, took on the challenge, diving in headfirst. The uncertainty, lack of clarity, and the knowledge that the work they put to the side was not going away inspired fear, frustration, and anxiety. Team members chose to view those emotions as signals to their opportunity to possibly support several nations in crisis. They worked effectively and efficiently to brainstorm their design based on a set of required specifications. Leaning heavily on their mechanical expertise, they successfully designed and built a model ventilator system that progressed into the testing phase. The model was a success! Not only did it operate as intended, but it was also superior to systems that were already available at that time. This team had, in the course of only a few weeks, designed and built an optimal ventilator system ready for full-scale production.

When asked how they managed to tackle such an impressive task in the throes of all the disruption and change throughout the company, the team lead made one statement that in my eyes made him a living example of a practicing Change Enthusiast: "No matter how tough the challenge, I know we can do anything!"

THE STRONGER THE SIGNAL EMOTION, THE BIGGER THE OPPORTUNITY

The entrepreneur always searches for change, responds to it, and exploits it as an opportunity.

— Peter Drucker

As I reflect back on my own entrepreneurial journey in the context of growth springing from crisis, my mind immediately goes back to 2020, the year that brought the world's economy to its knees. For me, 2020 proved to be the most challenging and greatest growth year of my business to date. I firmly believe one could not have happened without the other: My crisis enabled my growth.

When the coronavirus pandemic hit the U.S. in late February/early March, the live events industry came to a grinding halt and with it my monthly revenue. The new booking inquiries had all but stopped, and within just a month's span every engagement (keynote, executive workshop, and in-person consult) was either canceled or postponed. Like so many other professionals in this industry at the time, my calendar was annihilated. I was sheltered in place and feeling lost, not knowing how my business would recoup the anticipated losses. I spent nearly two weeks moving back and forth from the couch to the fridge to the bed. I was bingeing Netflix, Hulu, Vudu, YouTube TV, and any other streaming service I could find. I was devastated and needed more effort than I ever imagined just to engage in client calls regarding an event reschedule. Yes, that's right. Even the creator of Change Enthusiasm experiences the signal emotions of change. And on top of that, I was writing this book while my first-draft deadline barreled closer and closer.

It was at the close of those two weeks that I peeked out of the darkness and acknowledged just how loudly my signals were blasting. And it was then that I reminded myself that I am a practicing change enthusiast, and that these emotions were serving to wake me up to massive opportunity. And what opportunity 2020 presented! 2020 gave me the opportunity to share the message of Change Enthusiasm with thousands of individuals I would not have reached without pivoting into the virtual space. By moving my client partnerships from in-person to virtual using well-known virtual platforms like Zoom, Bizzabo, and Webex, I was gifted the ability to invigorate and educate individuals from all over the world in a single engagement without anyone having to pay for an airline ticket. As an example, I was honored to present for an online symposium that had nearly 20,000 attendees from every corner of the globe. 2020 gave me the opportunity to build and hone my home studio technical setup and virtual presentation skills. 2020 gave me the opportunity to hit the TEDx stage . . . twice. Both were uniquely curated virtual events attended by hundreds of people across multiple geographies. For 2020, I am grateful.

In the next chapter we'll talk about how you, too, can capitalize on the opportunity change presents through the practical application of the final step of Change Enthusiasm: conscious choice.

Chapter at a Glance

- Opportunity is defined as a good chance for advancement or progress.

- Trusting in the signal emotions of change to indicate the existence of opportunity and then exploring ways to capitalize on that opportunity is the second step of Change Enthusiasm.

- Recognizing something positive happening because of a past change challenge (growth, learning, new connection, etc.) creates a seed of trust that no matter how difficult a change may be there is opportunity within it.

- When devastation hits in either our personal or professional worlds, the opportunity to learn and improve how we navigate trying times is never greater.

- Change not only reminds us of our resiliency but invites us into a chance to grow even stronger.

- Our growth, in its evolutionary nature, demands intermittent periods of pain and struggle.

- When exploring the opportunity that change presents, it is beneficial to invite close friends or mentors into the process to serve as sounding boards and sources of differing perspectives.

THE CHOICE

Beliefs are choices. First you choose your beliefs.
Then your beliefs affect your choices.

— Roy T. Bennett

Brandon Sherman grew up in one of the poorest areas of New Orleans: the St. Bernard housing projects. These were low-rise housing units located in the 7th Ward prior to being demolished after Hurricane Katrina.

The youngest of four, Brandon was raised by a single mother who had a fifth grade education. Brandon's dad left the family when Brandon was very young and had never really taken an active role in his son's upbringing. Brandon was born in 1975, near the beginning of the cocaine boom in America. Crack cocaine usage was spreading rapidly throughout America in the 1970s and reached epidemic levels by 1984, with usage highly concentrated in poverty-stricken Black communities. Largely due to President Ronald Reagan's "war on drugs," which set harsher penalties for crack cocaine offenses versus its more potent relative, powdered cocaine, by 1989 one in every four Black males ages 20 to 29 was either incarcerated, on probation, or on parole, which contributed to the United States having the highest incarceration rate during this time period.[3]

---

3. *Encyclopaedia Britannica Online,* "Crack epidemic: United States History [1980s]," by Deonna S. Turner, https://www.britannica.com/topic/crack-epidemic.

The communities in which these arrests were happening were exactly like the one Brandon called home. By the time he was 10, he had already experienced close friends and family dying in drug- and gang-related violence. Every night around 8 or 9, gunshots would begin ringing out throughout the neighborhood. Every night. When people were killed in the streets, the police didn't come for an hour or more. Brandon had fights with kids at school who were seeking an outlet for their fear, anger, and frustration. That was his reality as a young boy. That was the environment that nurtured him.

One of Brandon's best friends through middle and high school was Monroe Gibson, known around the neighborhood as "Monty." They were two of the best players on the high school basketball team. Monty decided to pursue an additional extracurricular: the drug game. Because of this decision, he was able to introduce Brandon to the finer things in life. Monty had the best clothes. He had a cherry red Acura Legend with rims. He had the gold teeth. The gold chains. He had all the fine girls. Brandon saw this and felt a part deep down inside of him that yearned for the same.

Here. Right here. If you could put pen to paper and write the rest of Brandon's story, what would you write? Did he follow in Monty's footsteps? Did he do something about the lack of police presence in his neighborhood by joining the police force? Or perhaps he combated all the wrongful arrests by pursuing a more significant role in the government or law. Whatever you would write into Brandon's narrative would be based on *choices* you assumed he made.

CHOICE IS ONE OF YOUR MOST POWERFUL TOOLS

*It is our choices, Harry, that show what we
truly are, far more than our abilities.*

— J. K. ROWLING, *HARRY POTTER AND THE CHAMBER OF SECRETS*

Perhaps the most powerful tool in the arsenal of humanity is choice. The power of choice fuels our narrative. Every
day young Brandon sat in the seat of choice, and in doing so
was armed with the power to create his story, to create the
life he most desired. And the same holds true for you. When
faced with a lost job, a demotion, or simply a change challenge in your work, you sit squarely in the seat of choice. And
it's up to you to put pen to paper and write your narrative.

Our choices, in large part, create our reality. Take a
moment and think about all the choices you've made in the
past 24 hours. What time to get out of bed. Whether or not
to shower. Whether or not to go into your place of business.
Whether or not to smile at a stranger. When to eat. What
to eat. To whom to speak. What you spoke about. What
you read. Where you browsed. How much screen time you
granted yourself. How much time you spent with your significant other or children. Whether you took time for self-care.
Whether you stayed in or went out for dinner.

Those choices made the type of day you experienced
possible. These daily choices shape your life. Are you taking
a proactive role in your evolution or simply going through
the motions? Are you consciously enrolled in your journey,
intentionally living your values? Do your choices paint a picture of the person you know you were meant to be? When
in the throes of significant change and disruption, it can
become increasingly challenging to remain conscious, alert,
and engaged in our day-to-day choices.

When experiencing my first major acquisition (which I shared in the introduction of this book), I was drinking in excess, frustrated at the end of nearly every day, and simply going through the motions. Every day felt pretty much the same, with weeks passing by in a blur. After visiting with my mentor and allowing her words *bitter or better* to play over and over in my mind, I was inspired to reread my old journal entries. I could see in black and white evidence that I was doing the same thing nearly every day: wake up, go to work, come home, drink, eat, watch TV, go to bed, repeat. There was the occasional anomaly, like a weekend vacation or friend's wedding, but for the most part every day looked the same. It was on that day, reading those entries and hearing "bitter or better" repeated over and over, that I decided to take a more proactive role in the choices I was making each and every day.

When going through major change in your professional life, experiencing all the signal emotions of growth, it can become easy to unconsciously go through the motions. By that I mean understanding the bare minimum amount of effort required to maintain employment and doing only that. By "unconsciously" I mean actively avoiding or numbing out the stress or pain inspired by the change. But when you do that, you are not maximizing the growth opportunities into which those signal emotions are inviting you. The more you become consciously aware of your daily choices, the better enabled you become to grow through change.

The decision to take a more active role in my life's journey and seek a more fulfilling work experience began with creating and executing the exercise below, which allowed me to see where I was placing my priorities in life . . . and, by default, where I wasn't.

Exercise: Taking a Daily Choice Inventory

Materials Required:

1. Paper or whiteboard

2. A pen or pencil

3. A decent memory

Directions: For one week, at the end of every day list all the choices you made throughout the day, no matter how large or small. This exercise is about simply taking inventory of your day-to-day choices. When possible, note how much time was devoted to each choice and any feelings that resulted.

At the end of the week, review your list and group your choices by similarity, e.g., family, friends, health/nutrition, relaxation/enjoyment, self-care, money, purpose/passion, and professional relationship building. You can think of these buckets as your areas of focus. Take note of which buckets hold the most choices. Notice where you're devoting the majority of your time and where you are you making consistent choices.

Over the course of a week, you will be able to see where you are placing your priorities in life. In doing so, you will be able to assess whether what is reflected back to you is in line with how you truly wish to show up in the world. This exercise can help you assess your feelings, whether there are certain feelings that are more dominant in your days, and whether the more dominant feelings are the ones you wish to be dominant. This was a transformative exercise for me because who I saw on paper was not who I wanted to be. I was not living the life I wanted. Through this exercise, I created the data to not only support that conclusion but also to better understand where and how I wanted to shift focus.

Day	Conscious Choice + Consequential Feeling
Monday	Went to work for nine hours – Felt **blah**
	Led three meetings – Felt **excited** in the senior leadership team presentation
	Ate at McDonald's for lunch and dinner – Felt **blah**
	Drank four glasses of wine and one cocktail – Felt **buzzed**
	Called Rebecca (one hour) to see how she's doing with the new baby – Felt **good**
	Slept seven hours – Still **tired** after
Tuesday	Went to work for eight hours – Felt **okay**
	Took new hire out to lunch – Felt **good** seeing their excitement for the work
	Watched TV for three hours – Felt **blah**
	Made and ate dinner at home – Felt **blah**
	Drank four glasses of wine – Felt **buzzed**
	Went for a two-mile jog – Felt **exhausted** during but **pretty good** after
	Slept six hours – Still **tired** after
Wednesday	Went to work for nine hours – Felt **blah**
	Worked on big project due next week (4.5 hours) – Felt **blah**
	Ate leftovers for lunch – Felt **proud** that I cooked for myself
	Went out to dinner with friends (two hours) – So much **fun**! Felt **excitement** and **joy**
	Watched TV for two hours – Felt **blah**
	Drank three glasses of wine and four cocktails – Felt **drunk**
	Slept six hours – Still **tired** after
	Didn't start reading that book like I wanted to – Felt **disappointed** in myself

Putting It into Practice: A Manager of Others Handling Significant Resource Attrition

Vanette's Story

I've worked for my company for 22 years. I'm a manager of a system maintenance team and have been managing others for 12 years. My department consists of two teams: Team A and Team B. Each team has a team lead and a quality analyst. The lead of Team B was scheduled to retire at the end of 2021 and we had planned for our quality analyst to take on some of this team lead's responsibilities. We had a plan . . . or so we thought.

When the COVID-19 pandemic hit, it impacted many of our customers, which we expected would impact our company, so executive leadership decided to take action. To offset some of the uncertainty, the company issued a voluntary separation offer (VSO). My Team B lead took the VSO, which was, of course, no surprise, and I was prepared. Shortly thereafter my Team A lead took a position in another department. Surprisingly, I still didn't feel fear or any other signal emotions. Then our quality analyst from Team A decided to take the VSO. Yet again, I still didn't panic because Team A had another resource trained to do quality. But then my senior director announced that she was taking the VSO. At that point, my chest started feeling tight and I found myself feeling a sense of abandonment. Then I was told by my immediate director that she, too, was taking the VSO. Then, my quality analyst from Team B completely blindsided me by also taking the VSO. Then, one of the departments in our division got transferred out of IT and consolidated into our operation. With all of these changes falling one on top of the next—combined with the difficulty I had already been experiencing due to the pandemic, the horrific death of George Floyd, and other racial injustices happening across the nation—I found myself feeling afraid and extremely anxious. Everything was changing.

I reflected on the strategy of Change Enthusiasm and how it could serve me. I was clearly in the first step, feeling my signals. My emotions were all over the place: fearful, anxious, sad, frustrated, and angry. I felt like I was in a "storm of change."

Before all of this happened, I had been saying that I was ready for a career change and that I wanted a promotion. My department had become a well-oiled machine under my leadership. We were highly efficient and maintained high quality. I had reached the point of needing to admit to myself that I had become complacent with my current role. It was then, recognizing and embracing my signal emotions and sitting in that change storm, that I accepted the invitation into the second step—the opportunity. I remembered the importance when practicing this mindset of not getting stuck in my emotions, to get better not bitter. I started thinking that sometimes God brings storms to clear a path and that the storm I was experiencing was my opportunity to pursue other jobs. I recognized my options to be either drowning in the storm or sailing forth toward growth. I confidently moved forth into the third step of Change Enthusiasm and chose growth.

In that choice, I realized the VSO left several positions available ripe with opportunity for me to grow. I soon began feeling better about all of the changes going on around me, having decided to take an active role in developing myself and preparing for my next opportunity. I got excited and focused my energy into positive thoughts, actions, and emotions. I felt confident, not fearful. I made a development plan and listed my goals along with the steps required to achieve them.

Through the practice of Change Enthusiasm, whenever I'm faced with a change, I look for the opportunities that are available. Practicing this mindset is extremely important. Sitting in our emotions for an extended period of time will not affect whatever change that is happening.

In fact, we cripple ourselves when we marinate in negative thoughts and emotions for too long. We can either get bitter or better. We can take perceived lemons and make lemonade. This mindset has helped me navigate change with a positive outlook, and I'm grateful.

CHOICES CO-CREATE THE NARRATIVE OF YOUR STORY

Choices are the hinges of destiny.

— Edwin Markham

I began this chapter with Brandon's story, asking you to complete his narrative. Have you been wondering what Brandon actually chose? Today Brandon, through the power of choice, is a well-respected executive in the finance industry. He sits on several corporate and business association boards and is an active leader in his community. Brandon embraces his power of choice each and every day and I'm proud to call him a friend.

Back in high school, despite being intoxicated by Monty's gold and girls, Brandon chose the road less traveled, less popular, less fun, and less glamorous. Brandon chose to be guided by what he trusted would be a better, brighter future. He had seen the future play out for those in the drug game: death, jail, or paralyzed from a bullet. With long-term vision and a relentless desire for long-term fulfillment, Brandon chose to continue focusing on his schoolwork. He chose to continue engaging with his church community. He chose to continue exploring the extracurriculars his mom introduced him to like gymnastics, basketball, clarinet, and drums. Not pursuing the drug game is the conscious and most pivotal choice he made every day. By choosing to invest in himself, to invest in an education, he created the narrative of his long-term betterment. Sadly, his friend Monty was killed in a club at the age of 17. The return on Brandon's investment turned out to be life itself.

What fueled his choice, what inspired that intuition for better, was a chance encounter with a door-to-door insurance salesman at a young age. Brandon tells of the time a well-dressed white man with a briefcase came into his neighborhood looking for ways to help those in the community, including his mom. He remembered looking up at the salesman as a model of success not only because of his appearance, but because of his willingness and openness to see ability in everyone, even those far less fortunate than he. And in that moment, a seed was a planted. A seed of what's possible. A seed of desire to help those less fortunate. A seed of longing for what Brandon now viewed as the picture of success. A seed of belief, instilling the mantra "I can become something better" within him.

Now, there are things that happen in life completely outside of our control: Your company downsizes and leaves you without a job; you're surprised by a new baby on the way and in the short term must continue in your current job, which you hate, for the financial stability; you get a new manager with whom you can't seem to gel; or you are given twice as many responsibilities with no additional support.

The dance among the circumstance, events, or happenings outside of our control and our response to them defines how we co-create a life. Within the dynamic we create when dealing with those things we can control and those things we cannot lies the excitement, the tension through which growth is made possible. Brandon's dance was with the environment in which he was born, the influences and influencers in his surroundings, and his choices to focus on his schoolwork, music, and church. Many times in our professional careers our dance partners are those big changes that seem to blindside us, knocking us to our knees out of nowhere. Those changes that leave us feeling desperate, frustrated, and lost. The changes that stir all those wonderful signal emotions. The dance begins with our first chosen response.

WHEN OUR CIRCUMSTANCE FALLS OUTSIDE OF OUR CONTROL

Somewhere in yourself you have to realize—you are responsible for what happens to you. You cannot blame anybody for it.

— JAMES BALDWIN

When it was announced that my organization was being acquired and that my role wasn't guaranteed, it would have been easy to complain that it was all happening *to* me. It would have been easy to blame leadership for being inept. It would have been easy to blame my manager for not being able to guarantee I would keep my position. But any reward from playing the blame game is fleeting and choosing to engage in it would have been unproductive toward long-term betterment. Instead I chose to view the acquisition as happening *for* me. I chose to consciously enroll in the growth opportunities being signaled. And trust me, it wasn't easy. Trusting and embracing that stressful and challenging change happens *for* you rarely is.

One of the questions I'm met with often in my work is *how to choose better* when a change or disruption is so dire, so stressful, that the choice to get out of bed becomes increasingly more difficult with each passing day. When the best you can do in a day is get up, shower, and relocate to the couch. I know this feeling. Trust me. As I've shared in previous chapters, I've been there. These are the times when those signal emotions of change are blasting the loudest. When facing tremendous change or disruption, it's easy to default to going through the motions to avoid actively experiencing the discomfort and pain of uncertainty. It's easy to numb or ignore those signal emotions. But when we can focus on making intentional choices, we are empowered to use the magnitude of that emotional energy toward growth. To exemplify this, let's reflect more on Brandon's journey.

Though Brandon had a childhood filled with struggle and trauma, the most challenging year of his life was 2005. Brandon's definition of success while growing up was simply not living in poverty. Success was the ability to eat what he wanted. Success was the ability to live where he wanted. Success was the ability to buy what he wanted. By 2005 he was assistant vice president of a bank, in other words the right-hand man to the president. He was earning a big salary that afforded him a comfortable living by any measure. In all respects he had made it. He had achieved his original notion of success. Then in 2005 all the following happened:

His mother passed away from liver cancer.

His sister passed away from sickle cell anemia at only 27 years old.

He discovered that his youngest daughter had cerebral palsy and permanent brain damage.

He lost his job and home to Hurricane Katrina and was washed out financially.

He was mad at God, mad at the world, mad at life, mad at everything and everybody. In that one year he experienced more loss and tragedy than in his entire lifetime combined up to that point. It devasted him. He got up, ate, went to sleep. He got up, ate, went to sleep. For days and weeks on end. But as time passed, he tired of that routine and something turned over within him. It was in the darkest of moments that he once again embraced the power of choice: Get bitter or get better. Become a victim or become the victor. And one day he asked himself, Brandon, which will you choose? His answer was to choose to fight for a future he knew he was destined to live. Brandon once again chose life itself.

This dark experience taught him his greatest lesson: The storm does not come to destroy you, it comes to save you. The storms, our toughest change challenges, arrive to save us from what we thought was important. They come to save us from what we thought life was. In the eye of Brandon's storm, he was able to see clearly that he had been dying to live but losing at life. By striving to live up to his then model of success, he was losing at being truly fulfilled. It was only when everything was taken from him that he was free to reconsider who he was and what he was. Subsequently, he chose to redefine success for himself. Through the devastation and loss outside of his control, he came to understand and embrace his mission of helping people, restoring lives, and shaping the future. Now he is driven by this mission. Not by money. Not by the car he drives. And certainly not by the materialistic things he owns.

Brandon teaches us that when we are in our darkest storm to have tenacious hope and never be convinced that our story *ends* in that storm. He believed there was more to his life than his storm. In the creation of your own story, choose not to place a period in the current sentence, but rather a comma or semicolon. Then get about the business of writing the next chapter. Brandon did this by continually asking himself, Okay, so now what, Brandon? What's your next step?

In that question is where we regain our control. We may not have direct control over the circumstance, but we have full and complete control over how we *choose* to experience that circumstance. We have control over whether we allow ourselves to recognize the opportunities being presented or sink into the downward spiral, holding on to emotions that fuel higher and higher levels of stress.

In these moments, applying Brandon's greatest lesson is never more powerful: **Your storm has not come to destroy you, it has come to save you**. It's up to you whether or not you'll choose to take the hand of opportunity that is reaching out through the storm.

BECOME AWARE OF WHAT FUELS YOUR DECISIONS

May your choices reflect your hopes, not your fears.

— Nelson Mandela

When you're living in your storm challenged through change, being aware of what's driving your decisions is critical and can mean the difference between a better and bitter experience.

I can remember sitting in my manager's office as a young engineer leading my very first product innovation launch. My manager had just had a one-on-one with our VP in which she was told we had to accelerate our technical execution to expedite the product launch date. This was a major change to our plans, with serious implications and high risk. As my manager relayed the news and began brainstorming plans, I could see her overwhelm and exasperation. This incredibly accomplished and polished leader who was the best manager I've ever had, was visibly overcome by the signal emotions of change, which hindered her ability to make effective decisions and provide actionable directives. We wrapped up the discussion with a rough action list, but I walked out of our meeting feeling confused and almost as overwhelmed as she appeared.

A few hours later, she came to my office breathing easier and looking at me with steady, bright eyes. She asked to review what we had discussed earlier and ended up modifying some items and providing greater clarity on others. Somewhere during that second connect, we both expressed our overwhelm and frustration with the situation. I felt comfortable sharing after she had shown her own vulnerability by expressing the emotions she was experiencing during our earlier chat. I didn't have the language for it at the time, but together we were recognizing our signal emotions and embracing the opportunity before us. She wasn't inviting me into a venting session and the downward spiral that was sure to follow. Rather, she was walking hand in hand with me through the first two steps of Change Enthusiasm—step one, embracing the emotion as a signal to growth, and step two, exploring the opportunity presented—enabling both of us to move confidently into the third and final step: making a choice to inspire a better feeling.

During those three hours between our initial discussion and her stopping by my office, my manager had chosen *her* better feeling. She had chosen to transform her signal emotions into fuel for growth. I could feel her excitement at being able to get into the manufacturing facility earlier to execute our trial work as she relayed the additional ways it would benefit not only our initiative but other initiatives the organization had in the pipeline. She reiterated the importance of assessing and detailing the heightened risks to the new execution plan and assured me she would set up time for us both to walk our VP through them. That was the conversation I needed to solidify the new plan and move it forward with confidence and determination.

As leaders, through the power of choice, we can transform what fuels our actions from growth-stalling emotional energy to growth-sustaining emotional energy, just as my manager did that day. Through the power of choice, our emotion, which is an infinite resource, can fuel not only tremendous personal growth but also breakthrough results across our teams and organizations.

GROWTH-SUSTAINING EMOTIONS

Match the frequency of the reality you want, and you
cannot help but get that reality. It can be no other way.
This is not philosophy. This is physics.

— ALBERT EINSTEIN

Emotion is energy that can fuel action. But it is the good-feeling emotions like joy and excitement that nurture our overall fulfillment and satisfaction in life. These types of emotions are often considered aspirational. How often do you hear others say "I just want to be happy"? How often have you said that? We yearn to vibrate in these good-feeling emotions for as long as possible. These are the types of energy—*hope, anticipation, excitement, joy,* and *gratitude*—that can inspire us to make and *sustain* a given change. These terms are defined in the Glossary of this book along with their relevance in the context of Change Enthusiasm. I recommend taking a moment to familiarize yourself with their meaning and relevance before progressing to the next section on transforming emotional energy.

EMOTIONAL ENERGY TRANSFORMATION

Emotion is energy in motion.

— PETER MCWILLIAMS

As a chemical engineer, I've studied energy and energetic principles. This has ranged from defining how to achieve the energy density required to create a homogeneous 12-ton batch of shampoo to removing energy from a heat-generating chemical reaction. In my engineering career I often calculated the amount of energy required to do work or achieve a desired chemical process transformation. But ironically it wasn't until I found my place as a thought leader in the professional change space that I became truly enthralled with using energy as fuel. Because it wasn't until this time that I embraced the idea of *emotion* being energy in and of itself.

Energy, in an engineering context, is defined as the capability to do work. The first law of thermodynamics, founded on the principle of conservation of energy, states that energy can neither be created nor destroyed; it can only be conserved, transferred, or transformed. Applying this principle loosely to ourselves as emotional beings, we can either conserve, transfer, or transform our emotional energy. All are made possible by applying the power of choice. Let's explore this concept more deeply by walking through a hypothetical change situation and how conserving, transferring, and transforming emotional energy might manifest:

The Change: You are notified your company is going out of business and you and 1,500 other employees have been terminated effective immediately. You are given instructions to clear out your desk and depart the office for good.

Conserve: You hold any emotion about the change within. You might share what happened with close friends and family but ultimately ignore or suppress any negative emotion you're feeling. You become increasingly irritable, wanting to do nothing but numb out in front of the television and drink.

When we choose to hold negative emotions within, we fuel higher and higher stress levels and all the physiological impacts that come with them. By ignoring those growth-stalling emotions we allow them to fester. Emotional conservation can lead to stress-related health issues such as insomnia and hypertension. It can also lead to short tempers marked by moments of spontaneous emotional release that may fall upon someone who had nothing to do with whatever incited the emotion in the first place. Perhaps you've blown up at someone—a friend, colleague, or family member—for the smallest thing, which required you to apologize shortly after for the overreaction? When we choose to conserve our emotional energy over time, we run a high risk of that pent-up energy being released upon others in unhealthy, unproductive ways.

Transfer: You call a few close friends and meet up for dinner. Over dinner you vent about what happened, cursing the company, its leadership, your manager, colleagues, and the industry itself.

When we choose to engage in venting sessions, we temporarily transfer our anger or frustration from one individual to the next like a game of energetic hot potato. In my experience, this is the most common avenue pursued when facing the failure, disappointment, and devastation that change can bring. It's the choice that feels most natural when upset hits us. But there is something to be cautious of regarding emotional transference. Though it feels good in the moment, its magnitude temporarily reduced, the energy always finds its way back to us. Have you ever engaged in venting sessions day after day after day with seemingly no progress made toward sustainably feeling better? It seems as if venting is the *only* relief from your stress and it's fleeting, requiring you to do it again and again. This is because that energy is simply moving in and around us, unchanged. Though it provides momentary relief, it does not enable sustained fulfillment and growth.

Transform: You recognize the frustration, grief, and anger you feel regarding your circumstance. You begin thinking about the many years you contributed to the company and the friends you made there and are thankful. You are confident that over the past several years you've developed useful experience that can be leveraged elsewhere and decide that after a good night's rest you will reach out to your mentor to brainstorm the next best steps.

Through the power of conscious choice, we can transform our growth-stalling emotional energy into growth-sustaining energy. We can choose to transform:

- fear into hope
- anxiety into anticipation
- anger into joy
- frustration into excitement
- grief into gratitude

It is atypical for these transformations to happen with one single choice. It is the rare individual who can move from high-level frustration to pure excitement with simply one thought or action. This is not what emotional energy transformation is about. It's about being emotionally self-aware, and by making one choice after another inspiring better and better feelings that fuel action along your path to your best self.

Let's walk through a couple of exercises aimed at putting this concept into everyday practice.

Exercise: Transforming Your Emotional Energy

Materials Required:

1. Paper or whiteboard

2. A pen or pencil

3. A willingness to learn about yourself

Directions: In the "Allowing Signal Emotions to Light Your Path of Opportunity" exercise in Chapter 5, you figured out how to reach a better feeling when signal emotions strike. It's in the third step of Change Enthusiasm that you now make your choice to effectively transform that emotional energy. The exercise below builds on the one in Chapter 5 as it guides you to identify the choice, resultant feelings, and impact.

Carry over the "Productive Options to Transform" column from the Chapter 5 exercise and put it into the first column. In the second column capture the choice(s) you deem best. In the third column, list any feelings that resulted in you making each choice. There are key questions to ask yourself here:

- How did I feel immediately upon making that choice?

- How did I feel one week after making that choice?

In the final column, capture the impact of the choice. Here are additional questions to consider:

- What did I learn about myself because of that choice?

- What additional opportunities were presented as a result of making that choice?

- What connections were established or nurtured as a result of that choice?

Productive Option(s) to Transform	Choice	Resultant Feeling	Impact

LEVERAGING VALUES AS CHOICE FUEL

It's not hard to make decisions when you know what your values are.

— ROY E. DISNEY

By embracing the Change Enthusiasm mindset, we can harness the power of emotion to fuel our growth and betterment. In Chapter 5, we went through practical applications that allowed our signal emotions to guide us through exploring the opportunity change presents. A supplemental method for exploring opportunity and transforming negative emotional energy through the power of choice is bringing awareness to and choosing to live your core values. When Brandon Sherman was in the midst of the darkest and most challenging year in his personal and professional life, what fueled his choices were his values. He chose to allow his actions to be fueled by his core value of helping others. By making choices powered by this value, he found healing, personal growth, and effectively transformed growth-stalling energy into growth-sustaining energy. Brandon chose service in those areas where he experienced the greatest loss.

Lost his home = CHOSE to volunteer with Habitat for Humanity

Daughter had cerebral palsy = CHOSE to volunteer with Autism Speaks

Mom died of liver cancer = CHOSE to volunteer with the American Cancer Society

My toughest years pale in comparison to Brandon's 2005, but I can relate to the hardship and the emotional waves that can ensue. I can relate to the power of applying conscious choice to enable personal growth. 2015 was my first full calendar year of sobriety. It was the first year I experienced struggle and the accompanying depth of negative emotion with full clarity. Experiencing emotional pain without numbing it was both jarring and invigorating. On top of actually *feeling* for the first time in a long time, that year I had more idle time than I knew what do with. It's amazing the time I found once I put down the bottle and shifted my conscious thoughts away from drinking, planning to drink, and recovering from drinking. I picked up time from the liquor shelves; under wet coasters on the bar; in empty, stained wineglasses; under couch cushions; on the glaring pages of "brew your own beer" websites; in the pages of fine wine and liquor magazines; inside innovative cocktail recipe books; from the bottom of the Advil bottles . . . the list goes on and on. With so much time and clarity, I was let loose to experience exponential personal growth. That growth was enabled by a conscious effort to *transform* my life above and beyond staying sober. I made the decision to create and embark upon a 365-day conscious-choice challenge. Each and every week I populated a whiteboard similar to the following:

Value Foundational & Steady	Daily Conscious Choices Populate Daily	Weekly Goals Populate Beginning of Week
Spiritual Fitness	• Attended morning service at Spiritual Living Center of Atlanta. • Read 25 pages of *The Untethered Soul* by Michael A. Singer.	1. Attend at least one spiritual service. 2. Read a book that awakens and nourishes your spirit.
Financial Freedom	• Put $XXX against credit card balance.	3. Pay down XXX credit card balance.
Purpose & Connection	• Completed blog post. • Journaled for 45 minutes. • Had coffee with new hire.	4. Author one new blog post. 5. Journal every day.
Physical Fitness	• Drank 64 ounces of water. • Ate fish and veggies, no carbs. • Hiked a mountain. • Did a 5K jog.	6. End of week weight: —— 7. Feel healthy. 8. Maintain or lose body fat.
Relaxation & Contentment	• Shopped at the mall. • Strolled through the park.	9. Make time for self-care (at least five hours total).
Family & Friends	• Called Mom every day. • Supported sister in her career aspirations.	10. Support family and friends through ACTION.

The goals were small milestones I set each week that I wanted to achieve as I walked the infinite journey of living my values out loud. It was a year of intentional living. I put focus and intention into making choices in line with my core values. At its completion, I and those around me could see how my life had truly transformed: I had greater spiritual clarity, I lost more than 40 pounds, I was more financially fit, and I had begun placing the building blocks for the next step in my professional career. Recall this was also the year of the announcement that Duracell was being acquired by Berkshire Hathaway, when I embarked upon my second multibillion-dollar acquisition experience. I was leading and experiencing tremendous change in nearly every facet of my life without my once best friends Cîroc, Baileys, and Jack along for the ride. It was only through the power of daily, conscious, and intentional choice-making that I was able to experience lasting, fulfilled growth.

The next exercise walks you through how to populate your own conscious-choice chart when leading significant change in your life.

Exercise: Values as Choice Fuel

Material(s) Required:

1. Paper or whiteboard

2. A pen or pencil

3. An awareness of the values you hold most dear

Directions: Populate a chart similar to the one below following the instructions in each column. In the first column, list a core value. In the second, write down each choice you make that is in line with the identified core value. In the final column, at the start of the week list what you hope to achieve as concrete evidence that you are living this value in your everyday life.

Use this exercise at any time, whether you're experiencing a change challenge or not. This exercise will allow you to live a life more in line with the values you hold most dear. By living your values, you will be intentionally creating a more fulfilled life.

Value Foundational & Steady	Daily Conscious Choices Populate Daily	Weekly Goals Populate Beginning of Week

In the application of the third step of Change Enthusiasm, we must focus on the choices we make toward transforming our signal emotions of change into fuel for growth. We also must allow our core values to fuel our choices both inside and outside the workplace. This ensures that our choices are not only fueled by a desire for a better feeling but that they are also aligned with our core values.

Chapter at a Glance

- One of the most powerful tools in the arsenal of humanity is choice. The third and final step of Change Enthusiasm puts you in a seat of choice—the sole owner of how you experience a given change situation.

- Though it can be easy to do only the bare minimum that is expected during change and/ or to actively avoid the pain the change inspired, by choosing that path you will not maximize the growth opportunities into which your signal emotions are inviting you.

- Taking a daily choice inventory can help inform you where you are placing your priorities and enable you to take control of how you are living this one life you've been gifted.

- There are things in life that happen completely outside of your control, such as losing a job or getting a new manager, but what is never lost is your ability to control how you experience these situations or events.

- Within the dynamic created in dealing with those things we can control and those things we cannot lies the tension through which growth is made possible.

- The growth-sustaining emotions of change (joy, gratitude, excitement, anticipation, and hope) not only inspire us to make and sustain a given change, but also a sense of fulfillment.

- Our emotional energy can either be conserved, transferred, or transformed, all through the power of choice:

  - **Emotional energy conservation** is ignoring or holding the energy within, which over time runs the risk of leading to declining health or emotional outbursts released upon others in unhealthy, unproductive ways.

  - **Emotional energy transference** is venting or transferring the energy from ourselves to another individual. Though this often creates better feelings in the short term, by simply moving the energy around it remains unchanged.

- **Emotional energy transformation** is recognizing the energy being experienced and then choosing actions that transform the *signature* of that energy into something else.
- When navigating a change challenge, you can transform emotional energy by bringing awareness to and choosing to live your core values.

RESILIENCY THRICE REIMAGINED

The first time I did an intense workout in Georgia Tech's Bobby Dodd football stadium, I got a nosebleed. I'm a little embarrassed to admit that so I'm going to indulge in the urge to offer justification. Imagine attending a football game in the middle of summer. It's hot. Really hot. It's the kind of hot that causes you to sweat even if you are doing . . . *nothing*. Now imagine you've been tasked to run hot dog orders to every person sitting at the very top of the stadium, one at a time. And then, imagine that for every fifth person you had to make your way up the stadium on one leg. That's the best way I can describe to you what my workout felt like. Tough, right? Okay, it's only fair to admit I was the only one laid out in the field with a bloody nose that day, but still. It was the most painful exhaustion I have ever felt in my athletic career.

The transition from high school to collegiate athletics felt like a slap across the face. Even though I played three varsity sports in high school, the intensity level in college was a major step up. I was on the track and field throwing squad, specializing in shot put. We trained every day, sometimes three times a day, with morning weight training, afternoon practice, and afternoon weight training.

Don't get me wrong, I enjoyed it. I've always enjoyed sports and appreciated the rigor and dedication it demands in order to win. My favorite part (besides competing) was weight training. I still enjoy the process of breaking down muscle fibers to strengthen them anew. I enjoy seeing my body transform through that process. As you might imagine, my very first visit to a collegiate weight training facility was special. I remember parking my car and getting out feeling a rush of anticipation.

But walking across the threshold of that weight room as an exuberant, wide-eyed freshman, I could feel my anticipation crushed by overwhelming intimidation. I was intimidated not only by the size, layout, and equipment of the facility but by the massive athletes working out there. I saw linebackers from the football team on the powerlifting platform heaving twice my weight above their heads, sweat and spit flying everywhere. I saw fellow track and field athletes sprinting on the treadmills at a pace and incline that would have swiftly introduced my face to the floor.

Once I received my training card with a specially curated workout for each day of the upcoming week, I was refreshed on facility rules and guidelines, then let loose on my first training exercise. I remember the familiarity I felt once I got on the lifting platform. I was about to do a lift I had done countless times in high school and an ease washed over me as my body went to work. All of my muscle systems knew exactly what to do and by the third set any feeling of intimidation had all but disappeared. Though my trainer did offer a few suggestions on my form, I was grateful in that moment for the power of muscle memory, which enabled me to feel that I belonged.

The phenomenon of muscle memory is made possible through neuron connectivity in our muscles and brain, most notably the brain. The part of the brain responsible for movement, mainly the motor cortex, develops stronger connections between neurons that serve as the representation for a given motion. It's because of these connections that the memory of how to perform that action is much easier to access. The more a particular motion is done through repetition, the stronger those connections.

What if you considered your resiliency as a muscle? A muscle controlled by your mind. What if the *motion* required to strengthen that muscle was the experience of change? The more repetition you experience with change, the stronger the connectivity of the associated thoughts becomes. And ultimately, the stronger that muscle would become. I believe that it is in the experience of change that resiliency finds its training ground. Through every change challenge you experience, you are presented with opportunity to reinforce that resilience muscle memory. With every experience, you are presented with the opportunity to plant or nurture those seeds of trust in change happening *for* you, not *to* you.

Just as our physical muscles are torn during strength training, so is our resilience muscle tested in the practice of experiencing change. Some amount of pain is inevitable. Pain is a by-product of growth. In a physical muscle that pain exhibits as soreness; in our resilience muscle that pain exhibits as emotional hurt. But the more we practice the experience of change, the stronger our resiliency grows and the more quickly we can recover from those really intense, nosebleed-inspiring changes.

Revisiting the growth cycle shared in Chapter 1, the promise of Change Enthusiasm is made manifest as the muscle of resilience is strengthened. The more revolutions you make in the Change Enthusiasm growth cycle, the stronger your resilience muscle grows; as a result, for any given change challenge you will spend more time in the growth-sustaining energy of change versus the signal or growth-stalling emotions of change. This will not happen because of your ignoring or suppressing your signal emotions, but rather the opposite. Your muscle memory will enable you to better recognize growth-stalling emotions as signals for opportunity.

Putting It into Practice: An Entrepreneur Struggling to Grow Her Business through Writing

Celeste's Story

I am a new financial planner and have been in my role less than a year. I still have colleagues who help me with questions, but I am mostly self-directed at this point and in charge of my own independent contracting business. Leading my own business demands wearing many hats: service marketing, customer service, data collection, data analysis, client investment decision guidance, investment implementation, progress monitoring, compliance, and booking. Some of those rolls scare me more than others.

Writing an article on LinkedIn was something I needed to do to help advance the business, but I was struggling with it. I do not mind writing. I post in forums, on Facebook groups, and in discussion threads. I also do not mind public speaking. I have been interviewed for TV and spoken to large crowds on a designated subject. But a LinkedIn article seemed much harder to me. I had had some good ideas, but I struggled with pinpointing my audience and coming up with the right content. I have trouble not feeling like an imposter. Posting original, compelling work on LinkedIn just seemed so daunting.

On top of that, I did not know how to write something to a large audience looking for financial advice. I have a much easier time with a single client or a group of a similar type of client. But writing something that would be relevant and impactful to a large, mixed audience was really hard for me, especially not being able to judge their reactions and pivot the message accordingly the way I can when speaking to someone in person. This was a place I had to really stretch outside of my comfort zone. It was intimidating and frightening.

After learning about the Change Enthusiasm mindset, I considered my fear being a signal shouting out that I had an opportunity to grow in this area. Embracing my fear as an invitation to grow, I realized something was holding me back: me. Working the first step of Change Enthusiasm, I identified the thought inspiring my fear to be *Maybe it will not be professional enough*. It was this bias or belief that was holding me back.

Striving to let go of that belief, I worked on the article for a while but I was still too scared to post. Still feeling that signal emotion of fear and trusting opportunity being presented, I began exploring options. I decided I needed an expert to help me with my first few posts and chose to reach out to a few. Because of that choice, I have been learning new techniques and have even reached out further for personal coaching. I'm feeling more and more confident in my abilities to author impactful articles.

I know I will have to practice this mindset regularly as this is a new profession for me that will likely inspire more fear and frustration down the road. But I trust this mindset will be one of my keys to success.

RESILIENCE CANNOT EXIST IN THE ABSENCE OF HOPE

The human spirit is so powerful but it has to have something to hang on to.

— ELIZABETH GORE

I've never been bungee jumping. It's one of those things I think would be fun and exhilarating, but I have yet to . . . take the plunge. Even without having experienced it first-hand, I have a fascination and appreciation for those who have and especially for those who do it at rare heights and locations, like the AJ Hackett Macau Tower jump in China measuring 764 feet above the ground.

Watching someone jump from hundreds of feet off the ground with nothing but a harness and a cord separating them from certain death is awe-inspiring. I love seeing the transition from free fall to that cord growing tighter and tighter until it reaches its lowest point. It's there where the drama of the feat is most acute for me. Will the cord snap or pull back? Am I about to witness another successful bungee jump like the countless others before it, or the horrific death of a complete stranger? It's the presence and response of the cord at the center of it all. That cord and its integrity means life or death. If our experience of change and the disruption it brings were a bungee jump, our cord would be hope.

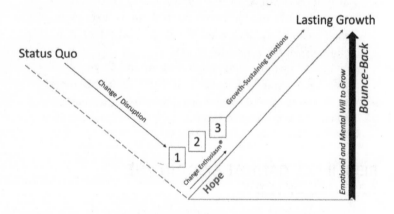

Figure 6: Disruptive change can take our emotional and mental state spiraling downward. During that free fall we find ourselves in the first step of Change Enthusiasm. In moving from step one to step two, hope begins to spring us up. As we continue the practice of Change Enthusiasm, hope and all the other growth-sustaining emotions fuel our bounce-back into lasting growth.

When change hits it can feel like we're being knocked to the ground or even pushed off a bridge in a free fall accompanied only by our signal emotions blasting through every fiber of our being. Resiliency or "bounce-back" happens at that lowest point when we *choose to allow* our cord of hope to spring us up, working through the first two steps of Change Enthusiasm: embracing emotions as signals to growth and exploring the opportunity into which these signal emotions invite us. Hope is the most critical of the growth-sustaining emotions, and it helps us to persevere through even the darkest times.

Elizabeth Gore spent nine years in the U.N. once she returned from the Peace Corps. The predominance of those years was spent working in refugee camps across Africa. At the time, the average camp stay for a refugee was 12 years. She remembers time spent in Ugandan refugee camps and seeing women with small children who had walked for days or even weeks to escape the horror and tragedy of their lives in Congo or Sudan. These women would step into newly created camps with the light of hope glistening in their eyes. Once rations were provided, they very quickly established commerce, schools for their children, and ways to get their hair done, which enabled them to present to the world in a fashion congruent with their bright, resilient spirits. There was more often than not this aspiration of making things better.

For Elizabeth, the most heartbreaking camps were those where hope no longer lived. Sometimes, she could see the light of hope dim from refugees' eyes. When that light was fully extinguished, anger and frustration would ensue. Individuals in the camp would turn on one another for the slightest wrongdoing. In the absence of hope, the camps became very dangerous places.

It is the cord of hope that helps us spring up from the depths of devastation and despair. That said, where does hope live? I trust that the light of hope resides within us but that it is only able to shine through the power of thought. In our darkest hours, we must be able to find those thoughts that keep hope's door open.

As you read those words, did the thoughts that keep hope's door open within *you* begin to pop up? What are those thoughts that generate hope within you? Is it a knowing that what you most desire is possible? Perhaps it's knowing that your children are living happily, achieving their authentic success? Or maybe it's trusting in yourself that in a couple of years you will have accomplished that one thing for which you yearn most? No matter the thoughts, find them and keep them close by. Identify those activities or places that inspire your hopeful thoughts, for example nature, exercise, or time with family. When times are tough, be intentional about engaging in and with them.

When devastating change hits, thoughts that inspire hope are the reinforcement that could mean the difference between your hope cord snapping, leaving you to free fall into a downward spiral of despair and anger, or pulling you up toward growth and fulfillment.

RESILIENCE SPRINGS YOU TOWARD YOUR GREATEST ASPIRATIONS

You always have to have something that you're pushing toward. The crap is going to come and it's going to try to push you, but as long as you keep moving toward your goal it's not going to stop you.

— Chaunté Lowe

Often those thoughts that swing open hope's door and fuel our resilience are rooted in the vision of the goals we have set for ourselves.

The first year of my business wasn't unlike the inaugural year of countless other entrepreneurs setting out to make their dreams reality: wrought with challenge and hardship. I experienced more rejection in that one year than in the prior five combined. I was putting intention, focus, and energy into building a consulting firm while working full time. I was figuring out the unique value I would offer and defining my ideal client. I was fortunate to have mentors in the industry who emphasized the importance of my being filmed speaking on stages to establish myself as a thought leader. That was the first time I had even heard of the concept "thought leader." If I had never even heard of it before how was I supposed to *become* one? Soon after I did some research and discovered it was something I aspired to become and had just been ignorant of the language that named it. I was continually told that having good video of myself on a stage in front of a live audience would help me to get more invitations to speak.

I offered to speak for free at any organization and association I could find. I strategically increased my presence on social media. I self-funded video projects, joined organizations of other business owners and like-minded individuals who were also pursuing the business of speaking, and attended as many networking events as my schedule would allow in hopes of finding someone to take a chance and invite me to speak to their organization. The "not right for us," "no availability at this time," "we already secured a speaker," "you aren't the right fit," and flat-out nos were coming one after the other. They were tiny disruptions on the path toward my goal of running a full-time business that would best allow me to live my life's purpose.

Those disruptions could have been the end of my entrepreneurial story. I was finding fulfillment and growth in my full-time corporate career while making a healthy six-figure salary. I enjoyed a robust benefits package and had a **steady** paycheck and **company-paid** health benefits. For those of you currently leading your own entrepreneurial endeavors, perhaps this resonates?

But with every rejection, I never lost sight of my goal of running a successful consultancy and impacting millions of lives around the world. Most important, the thoughts of attaining that goal kept the cord of hope stretched securely around my spirit. With that cord in place, my will and eventually my feet kept springing back up, enabling me to take the next small step toward my goal. Through the active practice of Change Enthusiasm, I allowed each rejection and resultant signal emotion to be a learning opportunity. These opportunities enabled me to revamp and fine-tune my pitch and put more effort into clarifying the unique value I brought to the table.

I reapplied what I had learned in my corporate experience regarding the power of branding to set myself and my business apart from the thousands of other speakers and consultancy CEOs. I shifted my pitch focus into seeking to understand client tensions and only then offering creative, *customized* solutions to alleviate them. Slowly things began happening. I began getting unpaid engagements here and there, which allowed me to create enough video to compile my first speaker reel. That speaker reel led to my first paid engagement, then the next, then the next. I started booking multiple paid engagements. I was successfully building my credibility and reputation in the change space. But please don't misinterpret the momentum I was enjoying in my entrepreneurial pursuits to mean the journey got *easier.* With success comes even greater challenge.

As I began seeing momentum in my "side hustle," in my main hustle I was tasked with leading the delivery of the biggest innovation the company had embarked on in more than three decades. It was one of those high-visibility, high-reward, and high-stress type assignments. Reading back through my

journals from that time, I found an entry that puts the experience in perspective (note that portions of the entry have
been modified to maintain anonymity):

*January XX, 2019: The day my mind nearly exploded. . . .
Sitting in an initiative core team meeting. One colleague starts com-
plaining about a process and then gets the most senior leader on the
call fired up. Then my manager asks me to set up a meeting to discuss an experimental trial that is coming up in a few weeks. After
that one of my direct reports popped in the meeting room to report
an issue that could shut down production in a matter of hours if
not addressed. But my mind was also on my side hustle. I was
waiting for two contracts for upcoming speaking engagements and
getting e-mails from another client about my next engagement.*

*Yeah. Mind nearly exploded. I'm sitting there in the moments
after the initiative call ends trying to wrap my mind around it all
while another colleague remains in the room talking AT me about
something much lower in priority that I have no control over. Had
to escape that room. Had to get out. Here at my coffeehouse haven
and I'm SO glad to be here. I don't want to go back. I feel overwhelmed. And disengaged. And I just want to escape. Leave. Quit
today and put all energy in MY business. QUIT TODAY. There's
something there. You got the signal LOUDLY today. Opportunity is
here. How will you choose in this moment? WHAT will you choose?*

Rereading that entry, I can almost feel myself right back
in that moment. I was so overwhelmed trying to manage the
demands of my own business while simultaneously managing the demands of the business paying my salary. That chilly
January day it all came to a head. It was through writing that
entry and putting Change Enthusiasm into practice that I
was able to transform my frustration into excitement for my
upcoming speaking engagements and anticipation of a very
successful experimental trial. Sitting in that coffeehouse,
guided by the goal of maintaining my corporate income to
supplement the pursuit of my entrepreneurial endeavors, I

went through the "Allowing Signal Emotions to Light Your Path of Opportunity" exercise in Chapter 5 to explore the opportunity presented. Armed with productive options, I was able to bounce back to the office that day focused and clearheaded.

Guided by a goal, inspired by the thoughts of attaining that goal, and fueled by hope and other growth-sustaining emotions, I was grateful to continue living my dreams. Today I am grateful I did not allow my story to end after experiencing so many rejections and disappointments in those early days. Today I am grateful my mind didn't explode sitting in that conference room.

THROUGH RESILIENCE WE OWN OUR NARRATIVE

Resilience is having a dogmatic mindset of not letting your story end in a negative situation. I have the ability to write my story for the better and there's nothing that's going to stop me.

— BRANDON SHERMAN

Perhaps the greatest prize of resiliency is the pen it hands us with which to write our narrative. That pen that grants the ability to not have our story end in rejection, despair, or devastation. Just take a moment and reflect on the beauty of that idea. Through the practice of experiencing change and integrating Change Enthusiasm into your life, your resilience muscle will gain strength. As that strength increases, you will hold the pen creating your life's story more and more firmly. You will become better prepared to own your narrative. You will become better prepared to maximize your opportunities, choosing learning and growth in your darkest hours. Brandon Sherman took firm hold of his pen back in his early years as he walked to his New Orleans grade school on blood-stained sidewalks so that by the time his storm hit in 2005, both literally and figuratively, he was prepared to keep writing his story for the better.

Picture someone who you consider one of the most resilient people you know. This could be someone you know personally or someone you know only through hearing or seeing their story. What is it about them that has earned them that badge "most resilient" in your eyes? I would put money on your response pertaining to some type of hardship(s) they faced and their ability to always weather the storm. When faced with a challenge, the most resilient of us have the ability to see the opportunity within it, to shine a light when no one else can even find a bulb, and to triumph over what are seemingly insurmountable odds.

They used the pen of resilience to own their history. But the truth is, you have your own pen. In the face of your hardship, struggle, and disruption you have the power to choose how you will use that pen. You have the power to choose what you'll write for yourself next. Will your story end or progress to the next exciting chapter?

Chapter at a Glance

- Resilience can be framed in three ways: a muscle, a bounce-back tool or spring, and a prize-giver of strength and the ability to own our narrative.

- Considering resilience as a muscle, it must be strengthened through the practice of experiencing change.

- Just as our physical muscles must be torn during strength training to regrow, so must our resilience muscle be tested in the experience of change.

- Pain is a by-product of growth.

- Resilience cannot exist in the absence of hope.

- Resiliency or bounce-back happens at our lowest point when we choose to allow hope to spring us back up.

- Hope is the most critical of the growth-sustaining emotions, helping us to persevere through even the darkest times.

- The more you practice Change Enthusiasm, the better and better able you will become to own your narrative and maximize your opportunities during the trying times of change.

PART III

THE
ADVANCED
APPLICATION

INTRODUCTION TO C.H.A.N.G.E. TRAITS

When leading and influencing through change in our professional lives, the skills that are most powerful are the softer ones that are not taught in classrooms. During change, the emotional complexity of a team or department is at its highest. Individuals are experiencing the full gamut of their emotions as they navigate through the change journey. It's during these times that leveraging the softer skills of leadership are critical to maximize employee engagement and well-being.

Shortly before ending my corporate career, I was leading the delivery of the biggest innovation the alkaline battery industry had seen in decades. It was a breakthrough battery design with new and unique ways of delighting the consumer through the user device experience. When powered by this technology, toy cars moved faster, DualShock wireless controllers for PlayStation 4 vibrated more intensely, and flashlights beamed brighter. The launch was highly anticipated throughout the market.

To add to the pressure, the development, scale-up, and launch was coming on the heels of the business being acquired.

After the acquisition transaction was complete, the newly appointed executives communicated that this project was THE top priority. It was known around the hallways as the "can't-miss initiative," meaning the committed time line for the product being on the shelves could not be missed without serious implications. This was a technology with a thousand times the complexity of any initiative that the business had embarked upon in the past three decades, and we had half the time to execute. I had 13 years of highly complex product launch experience under my belt across multiple businesses and regions, but this was by far the biggest challenge I ever faced.

Those working in leadership positions across the organization were, in a word, *stressed*. We were all still learning our new executive leadership team, acclimating to new systems, and knew this initiative was the opportunity to prove our capability and value to the company's new owners. If we wanted to set the stage for a long and fruitful future within these walls, failure was not an option. There was an undercurrent of tension in nearly every initiative team meeting and senior leadership update. It was as if everyone was waiting with bated breath for good news, that efforts were moving forward smoothly without issue. When issues did arise, resources were mobilized and charged with finding the right answers to ensure the launch did not fall off track.

I was responsible for keeping the technical team on track to deliver the volume of final product to customers when they requested it. I can remember feeling this tightness in my chest every time I approached a peer to request time from one of their resources to support the efforts. I knew taking time from their resources meant their organization would become even more constrained.

Though many conversations and meetings were filled with tension, there was one in particular that stands out where

I experienced most vividly the signal-emotion-inducing reality of those who lead major change and transformation in organizations.

It was one week before execution of the trial that would qualify the product for the market, and I was leading our key stakeholders through a readiness review with the full team. At some point during the discussion, the biggest stakeholder challenged our experimental plan and wanted us to include one or two other designs that the team thought up, until that very moment, would be postponed for a design upgrade post initial launch. As the words fell from his mouth, through the phone, and into that conference room I felt this overwhelming angst begin to take hold of everyone in the room, including myself. In a matter of seconds, I saw the faces of those sitting around me transform from confidence to bewilderment.

I took a deep breath, and I recognized my own signal emotions bubbling to the surface. Once I stepped into the opportunity, I decided we weren't going to figure out how to make the requested changes on that call. I plainly stated back his request to provide full clarity for everyone in the meeting and listed a few top-of-mind implications the team would need to consider immediately in order to fulfill the request. I then recommended we close the call early to enable the team to work through how to make it happen, reiterating full confidence in the agility, dedication, and capability of everyone involved.

The moment after clicking "end" on that conference phone is one that will stay with me for many years to come. You could hear a pin drop in a room filled with more than a dozen engineers, technicians, and managers. We all just looked at each other for what was in reality just three or four seconds but felt much longer. The deafening silence was finally cracked by someone sharing exasperation at the request, not understanding exactly where it had come from. We searched for someone or something to blame. We wanted to vent about the challenging position we found ourselves in. For several minutes I allowed that emoting to happen. The recognition and embrace of all the signal emotions floating in and around the room was critical if we were going to step into the opportunity and move forward focused and clearheaded.

As folks were filing out of the room, I realized something else was resting on their hearts and minds: the feeling of being undervalued. We had all stepped into that review expecting to be not necessarily applauded, but at a minimum recognized for all the work we had put into trial planning and positioning the company for success. It was resting heavily on my heart as well. Though it was a team composed of individuals carrying great resilience and agility, they were all feeling a bit deflated and uninspired as they left that room.

Once I had modified the project, I decided to call the stakeholder who had given the new directive. I updated him on our plan and shared my cautious optimism that we would be able to pull it off. He was very appreciative and thanked me for my leadership. But before hanging up the phone, I told him I had a request.

After thanking him for his leadership and recognizing and appreciating the tremendous pressure he must be under, I shared the impact his words had had on the team earlier in the day. I shared how after he gave the directive it was as if the air had been sucked out of the room. I reminded him of all the hours the team had spent over the past few weeks in preparation for this very critical milestone. The request I gave was twofold: (1) to provide dimension and clarity about what was driving the need for the trial plan changes; and (2) to recognize the team for the dedication, hard work, and restless nights put toward ensuring a successful launch. After he requested additional rationale for the request, he agreed to fulfill it.

He sent a message that evening to the entire team that reflected what we discussed. I noticed that eyes were brighter as we gathered the next day for our early-morning team meeting. The energy in the room had been transformed, inspired by the words and sentiment of that e-mail. We were once again leveraging the energy of anticipation, excitement, and gratitude to propel us forward toward success.

THE SOFTER SIDE OF EXCEPTIONAL LEADERSHIP THROUGH CHANGE

The greatest ability in business is to get along with others and influence their actions.

— JOHN HANCOCK

As individuals leading and/or influencing change in our organizations and teams we step into one of the most important roles in driving lasting change. It is our direction, our guidance, our feedback, our energy, and our behavior that can either inform and inspire or confuse and deflate those executing the change. I've reflected on that particular incident with that senior leader dozens of times over these past years. I'm confident he had no malicious intent in giving the directive to quickly change course in our trial plan. He was simply facing unprecedented pressure from the executive suite of the company and had to become more agile and flexible than ever before, rising to every challenge thrown at him. And so goes our work as leaders of change. We have to comprehend and communicate a change vision and remain flexible to changing demands from our managers, board members, shareholders, and investment partners, all the while ensuring our words and actions are having the desired impact on our teams and organizations.

Change happens through people choosing action. As leaders and influencers of change, we have the power to inspire those choices. It is people who make lasting change happen. Not systems. Not processes. Not slide decks. Not videos of CEOs talking into a camera. Not training manuals, standard operating procedures, or work-plan documents. It's people. It has only been in the past couple of decades that we've seen "people-centric" change management practices embraced throughout businesses and corporations around the world. Business leaders continue to evolve their change implementation practices based on continually learning what works and what doesn't. I have clients in the Fortune 100 with workforces of 100,000-plus operating all over the globe who are striving to become as agile and adaptive as their much smaller competitors. They are wise to the very real threat of a smaller, nimbler competitor being better prepared to respond to an ever-evolving consumer and customer market. These nimbler competitors have a true advantage in the face of market shift, an advantage that could one day mean running ropes around their large, wobbly ankles, ultimately resulting in their clumsy collapse.

What I convey to these clients through my consultancy work is the power of trusting that agility in business is made manifest through the hearts and minds of people. And as leaders it starts with us. This is the reason why the final portion of this book is squarely focused on options to enable you to become a more effective and inspired leader through change.

Whether you have direct reports or not, it is a leader's or influencer's responsibility to nurture, inspire, and inform those hearts and minds toward a change vision. Influencing action can happen no matter where you sit in your organization's hierarchy. If change success is reliant upon inspiring hearts and minds, then leaders must bring more to the organization than just hard-nosed, logic-based leadership skills.

The senior leader of that battery business very clearly communicated the trial change he was after, but he did so lacking empathy for the hardworking technical team trying day and night to just keep their heads above water. The result was a demotivated and uninspired team.

Change success requires us to hone and flex the softer, or more vulnerable side of leadership. This softer side is lined with traits like empathy, compassion, and appreciation. These are the traits we must use to open hearts and minds to our change goals. The softer side of leadership is how we engage and inspire others when they are being deafened by their signal emotions. Let's face it, during the dynamic times of change, emotions run at an all-time high due to heightened ambiguity and volatility, as well as internal and external pressures.

And it should not be forgotten that in stepping into the responsibility of leading and nurturing others through change, we must not lose our inherent responsibility to care for ourselves. This is something that too often contributes to the downfall of so many talented, capable, and well-intentioned leaders. We keep ourselves in the grind, ignoring or suppressing our own signal emotions in an attempt to keep our organizations motivated. The result is, we run ourselves ragged, eventually losing energy and patience not only for our team members, but also our friends and loved ones at home.

COMMON PITFALLS WHEN LEADING THROUGH CHANGE

Before getting into the more advanced application of the Change Enthusiasm mindset, let's first review the common pitfalls of leading effectively through change.

1. We diminish negative emotions.

   Often when leading change in our teams and organizations we acknowledge the change will be difficult but then immediately attempt to diminish the negative emotions inspired by that difficulty, not only to those in our organization but also to ourselves. The unspoken truth in business is that negative emotion is to be quelled so that one doesn't come off as "not a team player" or "inflexible." But modeling a "grit your teeth and bear it" mindset is dangerous because it ignores the very real emotion involved with change and can lead to employee burnout, disengagement, and attrition.

2. We focus too heavily on the change vision and corresponding roles and responsibilities, and not enough on employee well-being and fulfillment.

   Too often in the face of change, we view people as resources ready to be deployed against what needs to get done as opposed to individuals within a complex slice of humanity. When this complexity is ignored, it manifests into hurdles that stall progress along the change journey.

3. We don't fully embrace the fact that everyone wears change differently.

   Here's the simple fact: Not everyone is going to be immediately ready to jump on board and excitedly execute change. For any major change a range of emotions will churn across the organization, both negative and positive. When we assume a one-size-fits-all approach to change, we fail to empower our people to contribute and thrive in their own unique way. This fact must be embraced by allowing every individual in your organization the room to process the change with a bit of grace.

4. We don't provide genuine, productive outlets for employees to express and emote throughout the change life cycle.

    This includes, as best as possible, early engagement prior to beginning any change execution. When we, as leaders, do not create productive conduits for emotional energy to flow, we enable the potential for growth-stalling energy to continue churning within the organization through the rumor mills or street committees, eventually thwarting change success.

By slipping into any of these pitfalls, you could be costing your business millions of dollars in lost productivity and putting successful change adoption at risk.

In the following chapters, I'll introduce you to skills you should employ once you have mastered the practice of Change Enthusiasm. These are critical skills that will enable you to avoid the aforementioned pitfalls of leading and influencing through change. You will then be guided through exercises that will enable you to strengthen your unique skills. Use what follows as actionable options when in the second step of Change Enthusiasm to inspire calm and focus within yourself as well as any organization executing change.

Advanced Application Exercises at a Glance

Communicative

- Defining the *What* and the *Why*
- Driving Clarity of What's Expected
- Providing Feedback to Keep on Track

Hungry (Self-Development)

- Intentional Self-Improvement
- Active Self-Improvement
- Practicing Care for Self

Authentic

- Practicing Vulnerability
- Being Your Full Self
- Language and Behavior Congruence

Not Rigid (Agile)

- Stretching Outside Your Comfort Zone
- Remaining Open to Varied Perspectives
- Identifying Conscious and Unconscious Bias

Grateful

- Practicing Appreciation
- Active Gratitude Practice

Empathetic

- Organizational Pulse Check
- Direct-Report Engagement
- Listen and Respond

COMMUNICATIVE

The art of communication is the language of leadership.

— JAMES HUMES

James Humes was one of the most prolific U.S. presidential speech writers in history. He wrote speeches for five U.S. presidents, including Dwight D. Eisenhower, Ronald Reagan, and George H. W. Bush. James understood the power of language to move hearts and minds. James stated that the way you communicate, both verbally and nonverbally, is your leadership language. You create this language through words, the tone in which those words are carried, the frequency with which the words are spoken, and the facial expressions and gestures that accompany those words.

When leading teams through a big shift—when you don't and often *can't* have all the answers your employees beg of you—being intentional about your art or style of communication is crucial. Recall from Chapter 8 that *people* are the vessels that make change happen. And it is the power of language that can inspire and motivate the hearts and minds housed within those vessels of change.

A few years ago, my firm had the honor of working with a Fortune 50 client in the consumer packaged goods (CPG) industry. By the time of our engagement, their North American business had been on a change journey for several months with still many months of rollout execution remaining. The business was shifting brand focus, reprioritizing core market strategies, and implementing significant organizational changes. It was a major undertaking that impacted hundreds if not thousands of employees over several waves of change.

In one of my initial meetings with the senior-most leader responsible for managing the organizational changes, I posed one simple question: How have you engaged your employees in all this change?

She told me that a clear and robust communication strategy was the focus of their planning and preparation efforts even before setting out to make the changes more than a year prior. For this particular company, communication was everything. Their strategy included regular all-employee e-mail communications reminding the workforce of the overall change vision, the business imperative driving the need for the changes, and the latest status updates for those organizations impacted. They also held regular in-person meetings throughout the journey where employees were invited to ask questions and share their perspectives. This particular leader, charged with change-implementation success across several organizations, held managers accountable to enact regular check-ins with their direct reports to determine how they were managing the changes as well as inviting them to provide feedback on what wasn't working to share directly back with her.

These are effective, ideal actions for any organization embarking upon a complex change journey. The one dynamic to remain vigilant of avoiding is change fatigue.[4] When changes are thrown at employees at too frequent a pace, one wave crashing right after another, it can lead to burnout and lack of trust in organizational leadership having a clear plan for success. But when communication is managed

---

4.   Leadership expert Gwen Webber-McLeod, president and CEO of Gwen Inc., describes change fatigue as a loss of focus, energy, and willingness in leaders and employees constantly impacted by organizational change. Change fatigue symptoms include stress and high levels of fear, people not working to capacity, and distracted leadership. Source: https://www.nichq.org/insight/how-cope-change-fatigue.

at the right pace, the tension in an organization created by the signal emotions of individuals—notably the anxiety and frustration inspired by perceptions of being in the dark about what's to come—can be alleviated. As leaders, the more that we can leverage the art of communication to shine a light in that darkness, the greater the odds of inspiring our people into the opportunities change presents. This includes communicating when you have nothing new to communicate.

As an employee, when big changes are happening around you and your knowledge of their impact to you and/or your department is limited, anxiety and fear signals can begin blasting, growing in strength as you begin creating your own often worst-case narrative of what will be in the absence of real information. As a leader, the best way to support employees in this time is by (1) instilling trust that you have your finger on the pulse of the work being done behind the scenes, with every intention of sharing new information as it is available; and (2) communicating you are open to listening to thoughts and concerns and willing to address them as best you can given the information currently available. Acknowledging that there's no new information to share and then welcoming dialogue not only indicates your finger is on the pulse but it also helps to reinforce trust.

Having led organizations through major acquisitions, I know there are times when you don't have any information to share. During acquisition, there were numerous periods of time when information was either unavailable or I simply wasn't permitted to disperse it to the organization because of legal reasons. I learned quickly that maintaining two-way communication helps when tensions are fueled by the signal emotions of individuals who are concerned about losing their jobs and there's a perception that leadership is operating behind closed doors, withholding pertinent information. It's in these types of situations that even communicating that you have nothing new to communicate can keep a second lane of communication open—that of listening to your employees—and help to dimly light a path for others to keep stepping through their day-to-day.

Below are a few communication tips to apply when you have no new information to share.

Tip #1: Work with your senior leadership to ensure a robust communication strategy that includes regular touchpoints throughout the organization. A central strategy will ensure consistency of message across all organizations and functions.

Tip #2: If questioned about change status or what's coming next, be open and honest with your employees that there is no new information to share. Feel empowered to share the reasons behind it: You simply haven't received new information or are not permitted to share due to legal reasons.

Tip #3: Reassure every employee that concerted efforts are being taken up the leadership chain and when new and relevant information is available, it will be shared.

Tip #4: Restate the information you have and are able to share. Given the dynamic nature of change in business, be sure to underline the fact that it is the current, shareable status to the best of your knowledge at that moment.

Tip #5: Make the time to keep both lanes of communication open by proactively inviting employees to share their thoughts and concerns. Listen to what they have to share. Communicate your willingness to address their concerns to the best of your ability given the information available at the time.

Below is a series of exercises to help hone your communication skills. Step through each skill-building evaluation, rate yourself on how you're doing on this particular area today, then capture one action you're committed to improve. List an upcoming opportunity where you can take this action.

Give yourself a time frame and come back to capture the result. What was the short- and/or long-term impact of taking that action? Take an emotional inventory of how taking that action made you feel.

Exercise: Defining the *What* and the *Why*

Smooth change implementation becomes increasingly strained when change executors are armed with less clarity of the change expected, the *what*, and less understanding of what's driving the change, the *why*. As change leaders, it is our responsibility to communicate clarity of the what and the why to the best of our knowledge and ability. Complete the exercise below to self-evaluate your communication prowess in this area and create an action plan to improve. Then capture an upcoming opportunity to act on the commitment(s) listed.

Skill-Building Evaluation	Self-Rating (1 - 5)	Commitment to Improve	Timing	Result
I ensure the change vision and supporting business rationale is clear to my team or organization.				

Self-Rating Scale: 1=Never 2=Rarely 3=Sometimes 4=Often 5=Always

Exercise: Driving Clarity of What's Expected

Communicating expectations is critical to achieving your change goals. Communicating clearly what is expected of every individual involved or impacted in a given change situation can help circumvent unexpected roadblocks or stalls driven by confusion or misinterpretation. The exercise below provides you with the opportunity to self-evaluate in this area and create a commitment to improve. Once completed, capture an upcoming opportunity to act on the commitment(s) listed.

Skill-Building Evaluation	Self-Rating (1 - 5)	Commitment to Improve	Timing	Result
I succinctly communicate expectations related to change implementation to my direct reports, colleagues, and manager.				

Self-Rating Scale: 1=Never 2=Rarely 3=Sometimes 4=Often 5=Always

Exercise: Providing Feedback to Keep on Track

Once expectations have been clearly expressed, providing timely feedback to steady the course is key. This can be through positive reinforcement, when expectations are being met or exceeded, as well as constructive correction when expectations are not being met. The following exercise provides a prompt for self-evaluation and an opportunity for you to take action to improve. Once completed, capture an upcoming opportunity to act on the commitment(s) listed.

Skill-Building Evaluation	Self-Rating (1 - 5)	Commitment to Improve	Timing	Result
I offer clear, timely, actionable feedback with regard to my stated expectations.				

Self-Rating Scale: 1=Never 2=Rarely 3=Sometimes 4=Often 5=Always

HUNGRY

*You are your own biggest asset by far. . . . Anything you
do that invests in yourself . . . that's the best
investment you can possibly make.*

— WARREN BUFFETT

I had the pleasure of working with a client who was one of the biggest names in the social media industry. My firm led a virtual leadership experience with them in 2020 after the world had been turned on its head in the wake of the pandemic. As millions sheltered in place, this particular company was experiencing significant growth given the changing consumer habits and demands. But in spite of the growth, the company's leadership still chose to implement a hiring freeze because of the high degree of uncertainty.

Employees were being stretched incredibly thin dealing with the ever-evolving complexity in their work and the emotional drain of world events. My firm engaged their sales organization with a leadership workshop meant to arm every sales leader and executive with the tools to lead with exception through the substantial growth the business was experiencing. After wrapping up the workshop, I opened it up for questions. The questions were few at first, with many reluctant to share. But three questions in, a young lady popped on the screen stating she had a question she didn't quite know how to pose. She went on to share that though she didn't have direct reports of her own, she needed management advice about how to tell a manager to take time for themselves. She had seen many managers running themselves ragged trying to ensure their employees remained informed, guided, and supported, all the while neglecting their own health and well-being. She had seen fatigue manifest into short tempers and lack of empathy. This very important question inspired rich dialogue. Several people on the call, including myself, were so appreciative that she asked.

When leading change, managing multiple priorities that seem to be shifting constantly, and trying to maintain clarity and consistency of support to the people executing the work, we can very quickly deplete the fuel in our own tank. Warren Buffett, who will go down as the one of the best investors in the history of mankind, has been quoted more than once stating that the investment we make in *ourselves* is what will yield our highest ROI. There is no greater return than the time, energy, and resources we put into ourselves. Shall I remind you this is coming from a billionaire who has grown most of his wealth through long-term investing?

This chapter is about increasing your appetite for growth and self-development and feeding yourself when leading complex change. We must nourish ourselves if we are to inspire and motivate our teams effectively. Nourishment looks like taking time to breathe and check in with ourselves throughout the day. Nourishment looks like making the effort to strengthen those areas we most desire to grow and honing those areas where we already excel. Nourishment looks like taking time to recharge and relax. Nourishment looks like prioritizing the practice of our favorite self-care regimes (e.g., spa treatments, naps, baths, exercise, and long walks). When we don't do this—as I learned throughout my career and was reminded of by that young lady in my virtual workshop—those around us can be detrimentally impacted. Our *give everything we've got to everyone else but ourselves* efforts will eventually become counterproductive.

Below is a series of exercises to help hone your ability to nurture your growth. Step through each skill-building evaluation, rate yourself on how you're doing in this particular area today, then capture one action you're committed to taking to improve. List an upcoming opportunity where you can take this action. Give yourself a time frame and come back to capture the result. What was the short- and/or long-term impact of taking that action? Take an emotional inventory of how taking that action made you feel.

Exercise: Intentional Self-Improvement

Imagine that your organization must implement a new software platform. In spite of establishing experts both inside and outside the company to lead the training on the new system, you find yourself fielding questions left and right from individuals in your organization to which you have no answers. The frustration that situation inspires could be signaling you to expand *your* knowledge and experience of this particular software platform.

By intentionally searching for avenues to gain more knowledge and experience in areas where we would like to or need to grow, we become better able to support and influence others. Our areas of growth are limitless. We have the power to create lifelong, ever-evolving learning plans to nurture our continuous expansion. The exercise below provides you with the opportunity to self-evaluate in this area and create a commitment to improve. Once completed, capture an upcoming opportunity to act on the commitment(s) listed.

Skill-Building Evaluation	Self-Rating (1 - 5)	Commitment to Improve	Timing	Result
I actively search for ways to improve myself.				

Self-Rating Scale: 1=Never 2=Rarely 3=Sometimes 4=Often 5=Always

Exercise: Active Self-Improvement

This exercise works in concert with the "Intentional Self-Improvement" exercise where you began practicing intentionally searching for ways to grow and expand your knowledge and experience. This exercise provides accountability for taking regular action to grow. Complete the exercise below over the next 30 days. If the activity from the "Self-Improvement" exercise identified several areas for growth, feel free to populate an activity of learning and growth every 30 days for the next six months. For the results column of this exercise, be sure to capture how you improved a given ability or skill set as well as one thing you learned about *yourself* in the process.

Skill-Building Evaluation	Self-Rating (1-5)	Commitment to Improve	Timing	Result
I have something on the calendar within the next 30 days to develop my skills and abilities.				

Self-Rating Scale: 1=Never 2=Rarely 3=Sometimes 4=Often 5=Always

Exercise: Practicing Care for Self

For the sake of this exercise set aside any preconceived notions that may come to mind when you hear the term *self-care*, like it's just woo-woo jargon for people into yoga, chakras, healing crystals, and moon water. For this exercise, we are focusing on the idea that the term upholds: *caring for self.* There is no one on this planet with whom you will spend more time or rely on more heavily than yourself. How are you caring for that self? How are you appreciating that self when it stays up late during those restless nights before big presentations? How are you nurturing the relationship with that self to avoid internal arguments or urges to beat that self up? How are you having fun with that self, soaking up the best life has to offer?

Your relationship with yourself is too often neglected and put on the back burner when leading others through complex change. Yet it is that same neglected self who you call upon constantly to inspire and motivate your teams and organizations. When tensions are high and signal emotions are bubbling, this is the relationship you must prioritize in order to be at your best in service and support of others. Whether your relationship-building looks like taking 5 minutes to sit quietly after breakfast, playing a round of golf, taking 10-minute breaks throughout the workday to walk outside, listening to your favorite podcast on the commute to work, or biking 10 miles after work, it is imperative that you focus on it.

The exercise below provides you with the opportunity to self-evaluate in this area and create a commitment to improve. Be sure to capture an upcoming opportunity to act on the commitment(s) listed.

Skill-Building Evaluation	Self-Rating (1 - 5)	Commitment to Improve	Timing	Result
I take time for me on a regular basis.				

Self-Rating Scale: 1=Never 2=Rarely 3=Sometimes 4=Often 5=Always

AUTHENTIC

*Only when we are our natural selves is it possible for us to
project the power and mastery which is innate in us.*

— UELL S. ANDERSEN

I'll never forget the first performance review of my career.
I had been learning, growing, and contributing for a full year
after graduating from university and completing multiple
summer internships. I was an adult in the "real world" earning real money doing real adult things. I felt rock solid about
what I had delivered against my work plan objectives for the
year. The potential outcomes for performance reviews were:
did not meet expectations, met expectations, and exceeded
expectations. Before proceeding, let me be transparent:
I 100 percent fit the millennial mold with regard to being
obnoxiously hungry for constant feedback—especially positive. I was looking forward to every deliverable being rated
"exceeded expectations" and the fantastically glowing words
that were sure to accompany each rating.

The day arrived. I was ready to be praised and admired for
my exceptional work. Overall, the deliverable ratings were a
little less sparkling than I expected, with the majority reflect-
ing "met expectations," and only about 20 percent having
"exceeded expectations." But it was the verbal feedback that
completely rocked me. After walking through assessments of

each deliverable and reviewing my strengths, we approached the section of the review that targeted my areas of improvement. There might have been two or three listed but I remember only one: "Cassandra should learn to tailor her personal style to improve the impact she has in her work."

What? Tailor my *personal* style? Sitting in that office listening to that feedback being read aloud, I felt berated simply for being me. I was upset and felt personally attacked. Having spent years striving to be comfortable in my own skin, showing up every day being myself unabashedly held great importance for me (which, at that time, meant wearing ripped jeans and untucked T-shirts and saying whatever joke or quip might bubble in my mind at any given time no matter who may have been within earshot). It took me a few days, well honestly a few months, to receive that feedback the way it was intended. The language used was *tailor.* Tailoring is the process of making skilled refinements to something to optimize its fit without losing its core essence. Its *core essence.* Over time I realized that management had not suggested I change *my* core essence. Rather, the recommendation was that I reflect on how I was choosing to present myself and pursue refinement toward a better fit within the business environment.

To this day that remains the most poignant and impactful feedback I've ever received. Its lesson was twofold:

1. Remain in tune with your core essence and strive to always keep it intact.

2. Know your audience and how best they receive information. Pursue refinement without compromising lesson number one.

I firmly believe that by embracing these two lessons, your authentic self will be unencumbered no matter where you may find yourself.

Authentic self is a concept that has seen increasing use in the past few decades, with millions now consciously striving to bring theirs into all they do. So what is the authentic self? Authentic means being in alignment with what is true. For example, an *authentic* Persian rug is a rug made in Iran (historically Persia) with textiles from the region. It is authentic because it is aligned with what is true to its core essence. As an individual, being authentic means choosing to act, behave, and speak in ways that resonate with what is most true within you.

Wherever you sit in your organization, you are in that seat for a reason. If you have been granted a change leadership role, you were granted it for a reason. Trust that some part of that reason is to bring your background, your viewpoint, your perspective, your energy, your intellect, and your leadership language to enable success. The more complex a change, the greater the importance of everyone bringing their best, fullest, and most authentic self to the table.

This holds true not only for you, but for those in and around your organization. When varying perspectives and opinions are invited into the conversation, the chance of change success increases substantially.

By completing the exercises that follow you will help ensure that you are bringing your authentic self into your work and inspiring those around you to bring their authentic selves into theirs. Step through each skill-building evaluation, rate yourself on how you're doing in this particular area today, then capture one action you're committed to taking to improve. List an upcoming opportunity where you can take this action. Give yourself a time frame and come back to capture the result. What was the short- and/or long-term impact of taking that action? Take emotional inventory of how taking that action made you feel.

Exercise: Practicing Vulnerability

When your team members, direct reports, and peers are feeling their signal emotions and experiencing challenges dealing with a change execution, allowing yourself to be vulnerable demonstrates that you understand where they may be coming from, ultimately building trust and strengthening the relationship. If you are experiencing those same signal emotions, revealing those feelings and leaning into vulnerability is also living your true self. Not only will you be allowing that authentic self to shine, but you will also be inviting others into an opportunity for a moment of energetic resonance.

I do recognize there's concern that may be floating around in your mind right now: *If I show vulnerability to my organization, I will be perceived as weak, not in control, and ineffective.* To this I say, never mistake vulnerability for weakness. Allowing yourself to be *confidently* vulnerable with your organization takes more courage than hiding or shielding your emotions behind the guise of "I have all the answers; nothing ever shakes me." Understanding this is a delicate concept when in the context of business and the workplace, let's review an example of how to confidently step into vulnerability when talking with your team or a direct report. Applying this structure will help ensure your leadership integrity and authenticity is reinforced, not diminished.

First: Acknowledge the emotions being felt across the organization and/or by a specific individual. State plainly and sincerely that you are feeling them as well.

Example: "I can sense the angst and frustration in the organization, and I'll be honest, I'm feeling it too."

Next: Share a specific example of when you recently experienced a similar emotion and how you dealt with it in the moment.

Example: "I've been through several major restructures in my career, but this one is by far the toughest. Just yesterday afternoon I was so frustrated after our planning team call, I had to take a break to walk outside and clear my head."

Last: Restate again that you have had tough days. Relay that you trust in the benefit of making the change happen, calling out a few specifics. Reinforce that you will get through it together. Reinforce that you are there to support your team or direct report every step of the way.

Example: "But as tough as this is, I know the vision. I trust in the vision. Even though I have really tough days, I know once we get through this, we are going to be so much better because of it. More streamlined. More agile. More rigorous. More capable of handling the demands of the business. And please know, no matter how frustrated you may become, I'm here to support you every step of the way."

Take note of the structure of this approach and make it your own. The exercise below provides you with the opportunity to self-evaluate in this area and create a commitment to improve.

Skill-Building Evaluation	Self-Rating (1 - 5)	Commitment to Improve	Timing	Result
I allow myself to be vulnerable to my organization during complex change.				

Self-Rating Scale: 1=Never 2=Rarely 3=Sometimes 4=Often 5=Always

Exercise: Being Your Full Self

This exercise is all about allowing the truest part of you to resonate in your work each and every day. With your style perfectly *tailored* to maximize your impact on your organization, whether it's on your team, peers, or senior leadership, share your viewpoints, ideas, thoughts, and energy to enable change implementation success.

Another opportunity to unleash that authentic rock star within is sharing your passions or those things you're curious about. Wherever your passion or curiosities reside outside the office, be it baking, biking, rock climbing, or poetry, strive to find ways to integrate that into your work, sharing it with your colleagues and teams. Engaging in activity or discussion that lights you up can serve to inspire others in ways you might never expect. The exercise below provides you with the opportunity to self-evaluate in this area and create a commitment to improve.

Skill-Building Evaluation	Self-Rating (1 - 5)	Commitment to Improve	Timing	Result
I bring my full self into work each and every day.				

Self-Rating Scale: 1=Never 2=Rarely 3=Sometimes 4=Often 5=Always

Exercise: Language and Behavior Congruence

Have you ever had a manager who would say one thing but then turn around and behave completely differently? How did that come off? I'm guessing their incongruent actions caused you to lose trust in them. When those around us have to question who our true self really is, more often than not they will accept the answer to be in line with how we *behave* as a leader, influencer, and role model in a business experiencing change; it is imperative to shore up trust by aligning your words with your actions.

The exercise below provides you with the opportunity to self-evaluate in this area and create a commitment to improve. Once completed, capture an upcoming opportunity to act on the commitment(s) listed.

Skill-Building Evaluation	Self-Rating (1 - 5)	Commitment to Improve	Timing	Result
My words are congruent with my behavior.				

Self-Rating Scale: 1=Never 2=Rarely 3=Sometimes 4=Often 5=Always

<u>N</u>OT RIGID

*Leadership is an improvisational art. You may be guided by
an overarching vision, clear values, and a strategic plan, but
what you actually do from moment to moment cannot be
scripted. You must respond as events unfold.*

— RONALD HEIFETZ AND MARTY LINSKY

When leading change, remaining flexible and adaptable
to shifting priorities, new insights, new perspectives, and the
unexpected is a must. The most respected and effective leaders of our time, including Jeff Bezos, embrace the importance
of holding steadfast to a vision while remaining flexible in
its execution. Amazon's third-party seller business took three
attempts to get off the ground. Thanks to Bezos and his executive leadership team's realization that they needed to adjust
the execution strategy of this endeavor, by early 2019 this
portion of the business accounted for more sales than the
company's first-party retail business.

I've never been more aware of the importance of this than
in my work with a client in the consumer packaged goods
industry in 2020. Headquartered in North America, they had
been acquired by a multibillion-dollar European-based company about two years prior to our work together. I understood that post-close the CEO and her executive team created
a three-year strategy focused on seamless integration and
growth. Execution of that strategy was first disrupted about

18 months in by a major recall, which put unprecedented strain on their supply chain. After the CEO was able to shift priorities, deal with the recall, and begin getting the organization back on track, the pandemic of 2020 hit. She and her leadership team had to work quickly to protect the safety and well-being of their employees, enabling the majority of the workforce to work remotely while maintaining daily production in the manufacturing facilities. While still in the throes of making that happen, the company was hit with yet another disruption by way of a major IT hack. Once more, the unexpected demanded agility and flexibility in responding to immediate needs and shifting priorities while not losing sight of the overall *change vision*.

If at any time during the course of those two years the CEO and her executive leadership had stubbornly committed to both the three-year strategy vision *and* its execution, they would not have been capable of dealing with the major waves of disruption crashing on their well-intentioned shores. When we embrace that waves of change are possible and even sometimes required within a high-level change initiative, we become flexible to the ebb and flow of execution. Subsequently, we decrease the risk of our entire ship capsizing.

By completing the exercises that follow you will become more in tune with and increase your aptitude to adapt and adjust when leading change execution. Step through each skill-building evaluation, rate yourself on how you're doing in this particular area today, then capture one action you're committed to taking to improve. List an upcoming opportunity where you can take this action. Give yourself a time frame and come back to capture the result. What was the short- and/or long-term impact of taking that action? Take an emotional inventory of how taking that action made you feel.

Exercise: Stretching Outside Your Comfort Zone

A good way to hone your agility is, forgive the cliché, to get comfortable with being uncomfortable. When events or circumstances disrupt our well-laid-out plans, we are rocketed into the unknown. It's uncomfortable. It can rattle even the best of us. There's a reason that astronauts are required to endure extensive training prior to being launched into space. One of these trainings, lovingly referred to as "Vomit Comet," creates a microgravity or zero-gravity environment in a plane vessel, then introduces turbulence intended to mirror the jostling one would encounter during space travel. This is to enable the astronaut to develop a level of familiarity with what they will experience in their work *before* the actual experience, better preparing them to focus on the necessary actions related to the mission whenever that time arrives.

We can do the same to better prepare ourselves for the turbulence and jostle of leading change in our business. By making an effort to stretch ourselves outside of our comfort zone, we can gain a familiarity with being uncomfortable, training ourselves to be able to perform and lead effectively when that unexpected wave of disruption crashes on our shores. This could look like traveling to new places, trying a new sport, starting a new business, or simply doing something you've always done but doing it *differently*.

The exercise below provides you with the opportunity to self-evaluate in this area and create a commitment to improve.

Skill-Building Evaluation	Self-Rating (1 - 5)	Commitment to Improve	Timing	Result
I stretch myself outside my comfort zone.				

Self-Rating Scale: 1=Never 2=Rarely 3=Sometimes 4=Often 5=Always

Exercise: Remaining Open to Varied Perspectives

By inviting different perspectives and ideas throughout the execution of a given change, you will be opening a lid through which the experience and expertise of the organization can flow. With fresh perspectives, different ways of thinking, and new ideas your change efforts become better poised for success. Of course, there are circumstances when inviting several minds into the decision-making process generates a detriment instead of a benefit (notably, when you're under time constraints). But if you are continually making execution decisions in a silo without input from those who are actually doing the work, you could very well be missing out on the best ideas for an efficient and effective rollout.

As much as we may strive to be in tune with the day-to-day operation of our business when deciding upon the right change execution plan, we can never have the hands-on perspective and expertise of those who are in the trenches actually doing the work. One avenue to integrate in your planning efforts is strategically holding optimization sessions with the organization. These open sessions create intentional time and space to inspire and invite ideas and perspective on how plans could be altered or fine-tuned to improve effectiveness and efficiency. For example, you might hold one of these sessions after a major milestone in the change rollout to discuss what's working and what's not.

An alternative avenue I've seen my clients implement successfully is introducing either a physical or digital space where everyone can drop suggestions for execution improvement. These can even be submitted anonymously. Ideas from the most unexpected places have ended up saving time, money, and resources.

The exercise below provides you with the opportunity to self-evaluate in this area and create a commitment to improve. Make note of an upcoming meeting or discussion that will enable you to act on the commitment(s) listed.

Skill-Building Evaluation	Self-Rating (1 - 5)	Commitment to Improve	Timing	Result
I consider the perspectives of others as part of my decision-making process.				

Self-Rating Scale: 1=Never 2=Rarely 3=Sometimes 4=Often 5=Always

Exercise: Identifying Conscious and Unconscious Bias

When guiding and encouraging organizations through major change, we can get in our own way without realizing it. We do this by adhering to our conscious and unconscious beliefs or biases. Thankfully, identifying and acknowledging unconscious bias has popped to the forefront of leadership conversations. This is a relevant aspect of improving our leadership effectiveness through change, when emotional complexity is high. Our biases regarding the so-called right way of doing something could impede progress to the best possible solution.

When I transitioned into a newly acquired business to lead innovation initiatives, I had a strong bias for what I believed to be the "correct" way of executing. The correct way, as I believed it, included taking significant time in early-stage development and pilot design prior to moving to the manufacturing scale. This new business did things differently, moving quickly to manufacturing without having all the answers, trusting that solutions would be found along the way. Initially, my bias kept me from embracing that method. But over time, I began to realize that for less-complex initiatives, this strategy enabled the business to get products to market quicker than the competition. I was able to embrace a new perspective and establish hybrid initiative execution guidelines.

When we make an effort to identify, acknowledge, and understand how our conscious and unconscious biases are tethering us, we widen the path to the best possible execution to achieve our change vision.[5] The exercise below provides you with the opportunity to self-evaluate in this area and create a commitment to improve.

Skill-Building Evaluation	Self-Rating (1 - 5)	Commitment to Improve	Timing	Result
I take action to identify my conscious and unconscious biases to improve my ability to lead and inspire my team effectively.				

Self-Rating Scale: 1=Never 2=Rarely 3=Sometimes 4=Often 5=Always

---

5.   There are dozens of reputable providers of unconscious bias education and training, including assessments to help one identify their own. The online Implicit Association Test (IAT) has been self-administered by thousands as initial guidance. For more information visit: https://implicit.harvard.edu/implicit/education.html.

GRATEFUL

*The way to develop the best that is in a person is by
appreciation and encouragement.*

— CHARLES SCHWAB

In Chapter 5 we explored the concept of emotion being an energy. Along these lines, there have been numerous studies done on the frequency or vibration of various emotions. Across these studies, gratitude is consistently found at or very near the top.[6] It has also been discovered through studies involving magnetic resonance imaging (MRI) technologies, that when one is sitting in the energy of gratitude, the brain produces a higher degree of alpha waves. These are the same waves discovered to be predominant in the brain activity of monks during meditation. Alpha waves have been found to reduce stress and anxiety as well as boost creativity. Gratitude is a very powerful tool when sitting inside the opportunity that change presents. This is the reason this emotion is one of the growth-sustaining energies within the practice of Change Enthusiasm.

In Change Enthusiasm, when moving from embracing our signal emotions to exploring the opportunity into which those emotions invite us, one way to effectively shift the conscious thoughts that are bringing awareness to our signal emotions is to grab a mental hold of something for which we

---

6.   Suggested areas of exploration on this topic include the works of Dr. David R. Hawkins and Dr. Don Beck.

are grateful. I can't tell you how many times I've experienced acute signal emotions, taken a deep breath, and shifted my thoughts to three things for which I'm grateful. Taking that moment to shift into the energy of gratitude enables me to consistently bring my consciousness back into the present situation with a clearer mental space for decision-making.

But the impact of practiced gratitude is even more expansive as we think about leading others through change. When we can shift the focus of our gratitude or appreciation toward another, not for what they do but for *who they are*, we inspire and engage.

My firm led a leadership workshop for human resource executives across multiple industries with representation spanning aviation, consumer packaged goods, industrial/construction, and finance. When we began discussing the power of gratitude, one of the participants shared a story that inspired the entire room.

He sat on the executive leadership team of a Fortune 100 company. He shared that the company's CEO made a conscious effort each and every week to personally thank a non-management employee. He intentionally targeted those who were working in the trenches and gave them a handwritten letter detailing the specific effort for which he was appreciative. This required that he remain in tune with his leadership team on the good work coming out of their respective organizations. One week, this CEO chose a young lady who was in the department of the man who was sharing the story with my workshop participants. He told us that several days after he delivered the letter to this individual, he happened to walk by her desk and catch a glimpse of her wall. There, among several brightly colored sticky notes and printouts, was a prominently framed document. Upon initial glance, he assumed it was a degree or course certificate. But upon further inspection, much to his surprise and delight, it was the letter.

She had placed it directly in her line of vision when seated at her computer. That one gesture of appreciation continued to serve as a daily point of inspiration to that young lady.

Showing our appreciation for the unique value that our direct reports, peers, colleagues, and managers bring to the table is a very effective way of keeping the workforce engaged and self-motivated.

By completing the exercises that follow you will engage in the practice of gratitude to lift your energetic vibration through change as well as the practice of inspiring and engaging others through the power of appreciation. Step through each skill-building evaluation, rate yourself on how you're doing in this particular area today, then capture one action you're committed to taking to improve. List an upcoming opportunity where you can take this action. Give yourself a time frame and come back to capture the result. What was the short- and/or long-term impact of taking that action? Take an emotional inventory of how taking that action made you feel.

Exercise: Practicing Appreciation

Practicing appreciation effectively requires intentionality. Just as that CEO put focus and intentionality behind his handwritten notes, you should strive to share regular and meaningful shows of appreciation to your teams and colleagues. Strive to balance between appreciating individuals for *what they are delivering* (i.e., results versus expectations) and *who they are* (i.e., the perspective, style, energy, and ideas they bring to the table each and every day).

The exercise below provides you with the opportunity to self-evaluate in this area and create a commitment to improve. Be sure to make note of an upcoming opportunity to act on the commitment(s) listed.

Skill-Building Evaluation	Self-Rating (1 - 5)	Commitment to Improve	Timing	Result
I offer appreciation to someone in or around my organization every week.				

Self-Rating Scale: 1=Never 2=Rarely 3=Sometimes 4=Often 5=Always

Exercise: Active Gratitude Practice

When we introduce a regular practice of gratitude into our daily lives, we grant ourselves the opportunity to lift our vibration, reduce our stress and anxiety levels, and boost our creativity. But a regular practice must be just that: **regular**. Whether it be creating a daily gratitude journal or making a mental note of something for which we're grateful around the same time every day, our practice should be something we adopt and *sustain*. Having a regular gratitude practice will invigorate our lives both inside and outside the office.

During a leadership workshop, I learned of a unique practice that I enjoyed so much I've gone on to share it with hundreds of others. One individual shared that she purchased a fishbowl and next to it sat a stack of sticky notes. Every day she visited the fishbowl and captured one of three things on a sticky note: an activity that fulfilled her, the name of someone she appreciated being part of her life, or a food with which she was grateful to spoil herself. She then folded that paper and dropped it into the fishbowl. She did this every day for 30 days. At the close of the 30 days, once a week she would visit the bowl, remove a slip of paper, and, within that week, depending on what the paper read, either:

- Treat herself to a food she enjoyed

- Call or go out to eat with someone she appreciated being in her life

- Do an activity that fulfilled her

Once the bowl was depleted, she started her 30-day exercise all over again. It was a fun way for her to practice gratitude and fill her cup on a regular basis. The exercise below provides you with the opportunity to self-evaluate in this area and perhaps create your own unique gratitude practice.

Skill-Building Evaluation	Self-Rating (1 - 5)	Commitment to Improve	Timing	Result
I recognize the people, places, and things for which I'm grateful in a regular practice of gratitude.				

Self-Rating Scale: 1=Never 2=Rarely 3=Sometimes 4=Often 5=Always

EMPATHETIC

*Empathy is simply listening, holding space, withholding
judgment, emotionally connecting, and communicating that
incredibly healing message of "You're not alone."*

— BRENÉ BROWN

One of my clients—a company in the health-care industry
—had recently announced a multibillion-dollar merger with
a competitor prior to my engagement with them. The merger
was estimated to nearly double revenue as well as the company's employee base, and essentially transform the industry.
Once the merger closed, the company would move from the
Fortune 100 to the Fortune 50. It was to be a major undertaking that would shake the entire industry. As part of my firm's
engagement, I led a workshop with their executive leadership team including the CEO. It was a small group of 15. I
started the session with an invitation. We went around the
table and each leader was invited to share any signal emotions and associated thoughts they had been experiencing
over the previous two weeks. By the time we got to the CEO
it was apparent there were not only strong emotional signals
in the room, but outside the room within the respective organizations of every leader.

They expressed their anxiety about the pending integration
and the work required to be successful, as well as the anxiety

and frustration related to leading their organizations when they themselves had limited knowledge because there was either information they couldn't share or that they simply didn't have.

The CEO, sensing the frustration in the room, then accepted her invitation. She allowed herself to be vulnerable by sharing that although she was incredibly excited for the integration because of what it would mean for the business and the members they served, she too had anxiety thinking of the year to come. She openly shared that she had just found out the prior week that she would maintain *her* role post-close. As she shared her feelings it was as if the room took a deep sigh of relief. Their signals were being heard, recognized, and shared by their peers and their leader.

Midway through the session, as we were walking through the power of empathy as a critical soft skill during times of change and transformation, the CEO looked at her executive HR leader and said, "Starting next week, I want to rebrand our regular weekly communication to 'You're Not Alone.'" She went on to emphasize that everyone in the organization needed to know her team recognized the *feelings* of the organization and that they were not alone in experiencing those feelings. Yes, times were uncertain, complex, and dynamic, but she was committed to working through them *together*. She encouraged the entire room to engage with their organizations on a frequent basis, allowing time and space for individuals to express themselves and be heard. She recognized that creating that space would go a long way toward showing the leadership's compassion for the organization.

Empathy is one of the most important tools in our toolbox for leading effectively through change. In Chapter 6, I shared Brandon Sherman's story. When I asked Brandon the *one* lesson he would teach the world, he quickly answered: empathy. His lesson would be rooted in teaching the ability to put yourself in someone else's shoes before speaking or acting. He believes the biggest tragedy of our time is failing to empathize. When we listen to understand as opposed to waiting for our chance to speak, such rich dialogue can follow that helps us learn about others and ourselves. Imagine how much more sustainable change could happen with that skill alone. Empathy is one of Brandon's most important tools to live his mission and purpose. Perhaps it could be yours as well.

Below is a series of exercises to help hone your skill of empathy. Step through each skill-building evaluation, rate yourself on how you're doing in this particular area today, then capture one action you're committed to taking to improve. List an upcoming opportunity where you can take this action. Give yourself a time frame and come back to capture the result. What was the short- and/or long-term impact of taking that action? Take an emotional inventory of how taking that action made you feel.

Exercise: Organizational Pulse Check

The overall health of an organization (job satisfaction, belief in leadership, trust in company direction, etc.) is commonly handled with annual employee surveys, but during times of change and transformation, you must ensure that you are finding ways to increase the frequency of check-ins with your teams and organizations in more informal ways. These check-ins will enable you to remain in tune with what direction is needed or lacking, alert you to any pivots from your original plan that may be warranted, and provide more personal updates and perspectives on how the change is progressing.

Though large forums like town halls can be useful to disperse bulk information regarding change status and direction, genuine connection happens in the hallways, over lunch, in the break rooms, and at the after-work ultimate Frisbee game. Ask yourself, Am I taking time to put myself into these conversations? Am I creating opportunities to check in with the organization in these more genuine, informal ways? Complete the exercise below to self-evaluate in this area and create a commitment to improve:

Skill-Building Evaluation	Self-Rating (1 - 5)	Commitment to Improve	Timing	Result
I do informal pulse checks on the health of my team or organization.				

Self-Rating Scale: 1=Never 2=Rarely 3=Sometimes 4=Often 5=Always

Exercise: Direct-Report Engagement

We all know the value of scheduled one-on-ones with individuals in our organization; they provide an opportunity to hear progress updates, reinforce expectations, and give feedback. The most effective one-on-one is a two-way street where the manager shares direction and feedback and the direct report feels empowered and safe to share their own challenges, failures, and concerns. Each party involved speaks and listens. Allowing individuals in your organization to be heard when undergoing significant change is a powerful way to build trust and maintain engagement. You can do this through being very intentional with the time: During every one-on-one, reserve time on the agenda to check in specifically on the change situation. Share that your intent is to simply have a better understanding of how they are managing the change and if there's anything you can do to support them. Complete the exercise below to self-evaluate in this area and create a commitment to improve:

Skill-Building Evaluation	Self-Rating (1 - 5)	Commitment to Improve	Timing	Result
I hold check-ins with my direct reports to understand how they are managing the change.				

Self-Rating Scale: 1=Never 2=Rarely 3=Sometimes 4=Often 5=Always

Exercise: Listen and Respond

When our own signal emotions are strong, when we are feeling pressure from our higher-ups to deliver a change vision, we can sometimes let those feelings cloud our focus and attention when we're engaging with others in and around our organization. This exercise works in harmony with the "Direct-Report Engagement" exercise. It is about stepping into your one-on-ones with the intention of truly listening and showing your direct report they are being heard by capturing one action of support you will commit to taking in a timely fashion. During your engagement with the other person, open the floor for them to express and emote by completing the "Direct-Report Engagement" exercise; ask and then *really listen* for at least one help request you can fulfill. In doing so, you will be proving to those in your organization that you truly heard them and are there to be supportive. Complete the exercise below to self-evaluate in this area and create a commitment to improve:

Skill-Building Evaluation	Self-Rating (1 - 5)	Commitment to Improve	Timing	Result
I *really* listen during one-on-ones with my direct reports and colleagues; I do NOT multitask; and I follow up with supportive action toward any communicated requests for help.				

Self-Rating Scale: 1=Never 2=Rarely 3=Sometimes 4=Often 5=Always

PART IV

THE INTEGRATION

CHANGE ENTHUSIASM FOR LIFELONG GROWTH

Change Enthusiast (noun): *(1) One who is inspired to grow by harnessing the power of emotion. (2) One who trusts the fear, anxiety, frustration, anger, and/or grief that change brings to be signals directing them to their greatest growth opportunities. (3) One who practices Change Enthusiasm.*

In the time it's taken to read this book, thousands if not millions of skin cells in your body have died and been replaced anew. Since beginning the journey, you have been physically changed whether you like it or not. And so it goes with change—it is ever present and eternal whether we like it, believe it, trust it, or not. And the best part about change? It doesn't discriminate. Everyone is fair game, no matter their creed, color, sexual orientation, ethnicity, nationality, political party, or whether they sleep on the right or left side of the bed. The question is, what will you *choose* when change comes knocking on your door? You are now sitting squarely in the seat of choice. Armed with the concepts, practices, and tools shared in this book, you have a choice: Begin putting what you've learned into practice . . . or not.

Can you remember a once challenging game, sport, or task that you've now mastered? Outside of those for which you had a natural affinity, what type of effort did it take to get to where you are today? Did you have to train or practice every week? Perhaps even every day? Do you remember how inept you felt at the beginning?

Whenever we engage in something new or unfamiliar, it takes effort, attention, and intentionality to gain experience and eventually expertise. Change Enthusiasm is no exception. It is a belief system, a system that cannot exist without its defining thought threads being woven over and over again within you through mental practice:

1. The growth-stalling emotions of change and disruption (fear, anxiety, frustration, grief, and anger) are gifts, a prized inheritance of our species not to be ignored or suppressed. They **signal** an invitation to grow and evolve into our best selves.

2. Once your signal emotions invite you into your **opportunity** to grow, it's up to you and the mentors, friends, colleagues, and family you invite to participate to explore that opportunity, milking it for all it has to offer.

3. Through the power of **choice**, you can transform growth-stalling emotional energy into growth-sustaining fuel for growth and betterment. Through the power of choice, you can own your growth through even your toughest change challenges.

The promise of Change Enthusiasm is made possible only by *practicing* it through every change, disruption, transition, and transformation life throws your way. When the growth-stalling energies bubble up, it's this practice that builds your resilience (i.e., muscle memory), enabling you to quickly recognize them as signals directing you into opportunity for growth.

If you are a reader who is ready to embrace and practice this mindset in your life today, here are a few tips to be mindful of as you go forward:

#1: BEWARE OF THE SHORT-TERM COMFORT OF ENERGETIC CONSERVATION AND TRANSFERENCE

Although bottling up your signal emotions may save you from difficult conversations, vulnerability, and actually *feeling*, the short-term comfort is not worth the long-term impact. In the longer term, this energy will fuel unproductive behavior, stalling your personal growth and the growth of your employees and business overall. The same holds true for energetic transference. Although venting feels great and may even benefit you in the short term, continued practice does not enable long-term sustained and fulfilled growth.

#2: GRANT YOURSELF GRACE

When your signal emotions hit, the first step of Change Enthusiasm is to allow these emotions to exist and in turn to allow yourself the grace to sit with them. Understand that however that may look for you is okay. For me, it often looks like ordering a tasty meal (or a few tasty meals) and binge-watching my favorite shows. I grant myself the time and grace to sit with my signal emotions, keeping a promise to myself that when I'm ready, I'll accept their invitation to explore the opportunity before me. This practice is not about rushing through *feeling* our signal emotions. These are gifts to be appreciated and leveraged, not squandered.

#3: EMPLOY THE POWER OF TRUSTED PERSPECTIVE

Opportunity is a matter of perspective. As much as you may try, you may not be able to see the biggest and best opportunity presented within a given change or transition. Inviting a few individuals whom you trust into this step of the process can be hugely beneficial to paint a richer, more complete picture of what's possible.

#4: EMBRACE YOUR OPPORTUNITIES AS LIMITLESS

When disruption rocks your world, whether it be a challenging relationship with a new manager, an organizational restructure, an acquisition, or a job loss, once you've accepted your invitation into the opportunity presented, trust that the opportunity to grow is boundless. Be empowered to explore what's possible, starting in your current role and expanding all the way out into other industries and ways of contributing as depicted in Image 6 below:

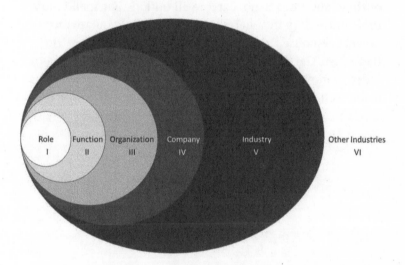

As you explore these options, there are three questions that I have found to be invaluable in focusing your effort. For change situations short of termination, consider your current company and role posing the following:

The company's values align with my own.
Yes ☐ No ☐

There is opportunity to grow and develop available to me.
Yes ☐ No ☐

This is a company to which I want to continue contributing my time, energy, and talent.
Yes ☐ No ☐

If you can answer yes to all three of these questions, explore options within spheres I–IV. If your response to any of these questions is no, explore all options but spend more time and energy in spheres V and beyond. If you are unsure of what response rings most true for you, spend your efforts there first. Get clear on the responses to these questions in order to move confidently into the boundless opportunities before you.

The Choice

#5: TRUST THAT THIS PRACTICE IS POSSIBLE EVEN WHEN FACING WAVES OF CHANGE

When waves of changes come crashing on your shore one after another, it can become overwhelming, even when you are feeling your most resilient. It is as if as soon as you have your legs under you with a marginal grasp of how a change will impact you, another change comes and pushes you back to your knees. But even when that second or third or even fourth wave hits you, your ability to practice Change Enthusiasm remains. As discussed in Chapter 5, the stronger the signal emotions, the bigger the opportunity presented. When faced with multiple changes at once, with high risk of overwhelm, segmenting each change and its impact can be useful. This makes the second step of Change Enthusiasm— exploring the opportunity change presents—more manageable. Below is a quick bonus exercise to help you transform any feelings of overwhelm; it can be used in combination with the "Allowing Signal Emotions to Light Your Path of Opportunity" exercise from Chapter 5.

Bonus Exercise: Transform Overwhelm during Waves of Change

Reserve 30 minutes in the day to add to the chart below. For each 30-minute session, focus on just one known change or one row of the chart. Couple completing that one row with the "Allowing Signal Emotions to Light Your Path of Opportunity" exercise for that specific change. To do this, feed the final-column responses of the exercise below into the first column of the Chapter 5 exercise. At the pace that makes the most sense for you, walk through every change row by row.

What Is the Change?	What Are the Known Details of the Change?	How Might This Change Impact Me for the Better?	What Can I Control in This Moment?	Associated Signal Emotion(s)

#6: MAKE YOUR CHOICES, THEN DON'T RUSH THE OUTCOME

More and more cultures around the world are evolving into those characterized by a yearning for instant gratification. If we feel bored, we want to either click a couple of buttons on the remote and be instantly transported into our favorite show or swipe up on our phones to unlock the bottomless vortex that is social media and web browsing. If we feel unfulfilled or unhappy in our work, we want a magic wand to swipe us right into a better, more fulfilling, and higher-paid job. But in the evolution to our best selves—consciously leaning into continual learning and growth through change—the outcomes of our choices take time. Instant gratification need not apply.

Practicing this mindset is as much about patience as it is resilience. You may face times when you want nothing more than to transition out of your current company or situation, and in spite of all the conscious choice-making there are no avenues in sight to make it happen while still being able to support yourself and your financial obligations. In times like these, the practice of this mindset becomes a practice of patience rooted in trust:

- The best opportunity to maximize my growth and betterment is hurtling its way to me.

- There is opportunity remaining in my current situation to grow and enable the growth of others; I can leverage where I sit today to grow into the best me I can be.

- I am learning and growing every day, becoming better and better suited to thrive in the next chapter of my evolution.

For the reader who is still unsure of or questions the value of integrating this belief system and putting it into practice, that's okay. This is your seat of choice and you're welcome to act from that chair however you feel compelled. For you, I'll simply offer a glance at individuals who once sat in that same seat and what happened when they chose to practice Change Enthusiasm:

A PHYSICIAN'S RETURN IN THE WAKE OF A GLOBAL PANDEMIC

A young physician just returning from maternity leave had to do so in early fall 2020 while the U.S. was still very much in the throes of the COVID-19 pandemic. With a young child at home, she was wrought with anxiety regarding her return. By employing the Change Enthusiasm mindset and its associated tools, she was able to begin transforming her anxiety into the anticipation of getting back to work and doing what she loved: helping and supporting others. Practicing Change Enthusiasm gave her the uplift she needed to step back into her hospital, confident and ready to heal.

A CEO'S ANXIETY TURNED SUPERPOWER

Elizabeth Gore, the well-respected founder and CEO you met in Chapter 6, has had challenges dealing with anxiety for many, many years. She says this incredibly powerful energy can either 100 percent impede or 100 percent fuel her. There is no in-between and no cure. It's been a lifelong journey bouncing from counseling to medication to various other coping tools. It wasn't until Elizabeth embraced the idea of anxiety as a tool in and of itself, rebranding it into her mental health superpower, that she began harnessing and transforming that power to fuel her growth. That growth included *choosing* to implement a mental health and anxiety resource center on the Hello Alice platform in 2020. By embracing anxiety as a signal and tool for growth, Elizabeth has become better at serving her hundreds of thousands of customers all around the world.

AN EMPLOYEE DEMOTED YET DETERMINED

A young contributor in the hospitality industry learned she was being demoted. In a whirlwind, she experienced all of the signal emotions of change seemingly at once. She recognized that the depth of the emotion she was feeling meant that she was sitting in one of the greatest opportunities of her life. So she used the time in the demoted position to learn more about her business and the industry itself, and mapped out exactly where and how she wanted to contribute. If not for that demotion, she likely would not have been signaled into defining what she truly wanted in her career.

A SENIOR EXECUTIVE'S DIFFICULT CONVERSATION TURNED OPPORTUNITY

A senior-level executive was facing a difficult conversation with an individual in his organization. This individual did not accept feedback well, getting defensive and making excuses for his subpar performance. Even though the executive had been a manager for more than 20 years, he was absolutely dreading the difficult conversation he needed to have with this employee. Thinking about it was causing him incredible stress. It was then, hearing his signal emotions blasting, that he decided to employ the mindset of Change Enthusiasm. He recognized that he had the power to choose to transform his negative emotional energy into fuel for fulfilling growth. He asked himself, What if I approached this entire discussion from the perspective of making myself a stronger and more impactful leader? He recognized and embraced this conversation as an opportunity to grow.

He went into the conversation feeling much more positive. It was indeed a tough one, made even tougher by having it virtually in the midst of the pandemic (which meant he was unable to really pick up on nonverbal cues throughout the conversation). The employee was quieter than normal and seemed less defensive. Over the following month the executive began to see improvement in the employee's performance. Through integrating the mindset of Change Enthusiasm, this executive became a better leader and a better inspiration to his direct report.

AN OVERWHELMED SERVICE PROVIDER WHO FLIPPED HER SCRIPT

The coronavirus pandemic found those in their senior years at the highest risk of experiencing the worst the disease had to offer. The exceptional care of these individuals became paramount in early 2020. One of those responsible was a U.S.-based service provider to caregivers throughout the senior community. This CEO had been contributing to the senior community for decades, pursuing her passion for compassionate and robust care. In the wake of the pandemic, she found herself overwhelmed by the growing demands and exasperation of her client base, which caused her to reach for her old habit of allowing certain tasks to trigger negative mental scripts. Through embracing Change Enthusiasm she was enabled to recognize and *name* that habit. She then made the choice to transform those scripts into growth-sustaining emotional energies, thoughts, and actions. She leaned into building her resiliency muscle, becoming laser-focused on providing her customers and those for whom they care with exceptional service during the most trying time of her career.

For those who have embraced this mindset, I have witnessed a transformation in how they engage in and lead others through change. I have seen senior executives reach heightened levels of emotional self-awareness, becoming more inspired leaders of thousands. I've seen individuals become more open, allowing their signal emotions to invite them into their exploration of opportunity to grow. I've seen leaders who are exuberant and fully empowered to choose their better: better work experience, better feelings, better and more effective support to their organization.

The promise of putting Change Enthusiasm into practice in your life is a stronger resilience muscle, more inspired and effective leadership, a more rapid pace into those growth-sustaining emotional energies in the face of disruption and living more authentically successful every day. So how about it? What will *you* choose?

GLOSSARY

20/20 change vision: A knowing and trust that opportunity to learn and grow lies within even the toughest changes and disruptions

anger: A negative feeling oriented toward some real or supposed grievance[7]

Relevance in the practice of Change Enthusiasm: The grievance[8] may be that major change or shift, which we perceive as happening to us. That change we didn't ask for and never really wanted. That change that just gets thrust upon us whether we like it or not. Often in the face of this type of change the energy of anger is stirred up within.

Synonyms: rage, outrage, madness, fury, wrath, ire

anticipation: Foreseeing or preparing for something in advance[9]

Relevance in the practice of Change Enthusiasm: Trusting that a given change has something good in store for us, the energy of anticipation can focus our preparation efforts to maximize the opportunity.

Synonyms: contemplation, expectancy, prospect

anxiety: Worry and nervousness[10]

---

7. Patrick Michael Ryan, *Dictionary of Emotions: Words for Feelings, Moods, and Emotions* (Pamaxama, 2014), page 16.
8. *Grievance* per Merriam-Webster is defined as "a cause of distress (such as an unsatisfactory working condition) felt to afford reason for complaint or resistance."
9. *Dictionary of Emotions: Words for Feelings, Moods, and Emotions*, page 18.
10. IBID.

Relevance in the practice of Change Enthusiasm: Anxiety is a very real and raw energy. When ignored it can lead to serious, adverse health conditions. This energy is often experienced in the face of change because the environment becomes dynamic, unstable, and ambiguous. This is the type of environment in which the energy of anxiety truly thrives.

Synonyms: agitation, apprehension, concern, uneasiness, agitation

change adoption: The act of embracing a given change, striving to live it day-to-day, committed to creating it as status quo

change challenge: A process, relationship, or way of working that is new or different from the status quo, rife with unknowns; it often invites discomfort fueled by fear and anxiety

change event: A happening, such losing a job or getting a new manager, that requires a shift from the status quo or the way one had typically done things

change fatigue: The experience of feeling disengaged from and uncommitted to executing and/or leading change driven by being overwhelmed by frequency and/or scope of change

change goals: The desired outputs from a given change, such as increased efficiency, improved morale, or lower cost

change journey: The path of moving through a given change, starting at the time of learning of the change all the way through comfortably living the change in your day-to-day

change management: A holistic strategy to achieve a given change inclusive of impacts to people, process, execution schedule, and cost

change situation: The set of circumstances surrounding a new or different way of working or being, such as onboarding into a new job or starting a new business venture

change success: The state achieved once all change goals have been deemed complete

change vision: A picture of what could be once a given change is successfully executed and adopted

conscious enrollment: Making a mental effort to actively engage in the events and circumstances in which you find yourself

excitement: Lively and cheerful joy[11]

Relevance in the practice of Change Enthusiasm: The energy of excitement when unleashed is so very raw. When permitted to run rampant, it can fuel our bodies into spontaneous song and dance. But when we can focus this energy into leading and implementing change, it fuels efficiency and creativity toward the best possible outcome.

Synonym: incitement

fear: Afraid, anxious, or apprehensive about a possible or probable situation[12]

Relevance in the practice of Change Enthusiasm: Possible or probable language in this definition means that the energy is made manifest not through reality but through perception of reality—an example being the perception of losing your job upon hearing an organizational restructure announcement. Or the perception of you being voted out of your C-suite position by your board once news hits of your top competitor stealing 15 percent of the market share.

Synonyms: dread, panic, alarm, trepidation

frustration: Annoyance at being hindered in attaining one's goals[13]

Relevance in the practice of Change Enthusiasm: Change can seemingly knock us off our carefully curated plans to reach our goals, professional or otherwise. When that happens, the energy of frustration begins to vibrate within.

---

11. Patrick Michael Ryan, *Dictionary of Emotions: Words for Feelings, Moods, and Emotions* (Pamaxama, 2014), page 123.
12. *Dictionary of Emotions: Words for Feelings, Moods, and Emotions*, page 131.
13. *Dictionary of Emotions: Words for Feelings, Moods, and Emotions*, page 143.

Synonyms: aggravation, annoyance, exasperation, hassle, nuisance

gratitude: Thankfulness and appreciation[14]

Relevance in the practice of Change Enthusiasm: No matter the situation or circumstance in which change may welcome us, there is always something for which to be grateful. Emotional transformation, a concept discussed below, is most efficient when gratitude is the aspiring energy.

Synonym: appreciation

grief: Intense sorrow caused by a loss of a loved one (especially by death)[15]

Relevance in the practice of Change Enthusiasm: Though we most often think of grief in the context of losing a person, grief can be experienced in the face of any loss of something that we held dear, such as a job or position, a high level of comfort in our day-to-day work, or a dream. Often our dreams are lost or vanish from the realm of possibility due to changed circumstances outside of our control.

Synonyms: anguish, heartbreak, sorrow, affliction, woe

growth-stalling energy/emotions: The emotional energies like fear, anger, frustration, anxiety, and grief that over the long term impede and/or stall individual and collective growth

growth-sustaining energy/emotions: The emotional energies of hope, joy, gratitude, excitement, and anticipation that over the long term accelerate and/or sustain individual and collective growth

hope: A state of belief that some desire will be fulfilled[16]

---

14. *Dictionary of Emotions: Words for Feelings, Moods, and Emotions*, page 160.
15. *Dictionary of Emotions: Words for Feelings, Moods, and Emotions*, page 151.
16. *Dictionary of Emotions: Words for Feelings, Moods, and Emotions*, page 162.

Relevance in the practice of Change Enthusiasm: The only difference between hope and fear is one's own expectation, perspective, or belief. Said another way, fear is hope in disguise. We have the power to banish that disguise and experience hope in all its glory simply by changing our expectation or belief of what's to come. When we can become hopeful about what a pending change could mean for us, we are gently pulled into making that change a reality.

Synonyms: aspire, dream, aim, allow

joy: Great happiness[17]

Relevance in the practice of Change Enthusiasm: To lead and implement change filled with joy is to lead and implement change truly fulfilled. Joy energy is a bedrock fuel, a steady undercurrent that promotes a willingness to act and achieve continual success.

Synonyms: bliss, gladness, warm fuzzies

leadership language: The style and content of speech consistently used by an individual to influence others

professional change space: The area of your work or business that is impacted by a change event or change situation

signal emotions: The five emotions commonly inspired in the face of major change and disruption, which invite one into their opportunity to learn and grow (fear, anxiety, frustration, anger, and grief)

---

17. *Dictionary of Emotions: Words for Feelings, Moods, and Emotions*, page 191.

BIBLIOGRAPHY

Andersen, U.S., *Three Magic Words: The Key to Power, Peace, and Plenty* (Stellar Classics, 2017).

Fuller, Pamela, Mark Murphy, Anne Chow, *The Leader's Guide to Unconscious Bias: How to Reframe Bias, Cultivate Connection, and Create High-Performing Teams* (Simon & Schuster, 2020).

Hatfield, Elaine, John T. Cacioppo, Richard L. Rapson, *Emotional Contagion: Studies in Emotion and Social Interaction* (Cambridge CB2 1RP, England: Cambridge University Press, 1994).

Hawkins M.D. Ph.D., David R., *Power vs Force* (Hay House Inc., 2014).

Ryan, Patrick Michael, *Dictionary of Emotions: Words for Feelings, Moods, and Emotions* (Pamaxama, 2014).

Saad, Layla F., *Me and My White Supremacy: Combat Racism, Change the World, and Become a Good Ancestor* (Sourcebooks, 2020).

Sterrett, Ph.D., Emily A., *The Science Behind Emotional Intelligence* (Amherst, MA: HRD Press, 2014).

Turner, Deonna S., *"Crack epidemic: United States History [1980s],"* Encyclopaedia Britannica Online, https://www.britannica.com/topic/crack-epidemic.

INDEX

ACKNOWLEDGMENTS

I am eternally grateful for the love and support of my family: Theresa, Gilbert, Tishanna, and Richard. If not for them, I would not be the expression I am today. For every trampoline double bounce (yes, even THAT one), vacation, innovative nickname, argument, Nintendo Power Pad cheat discovery, actor/actress debate, belly-busting laugh, and late-night movie marathon I am grateful. You all rock and you *know* it. To Reid Tracy and Cheryl Richardson, thank you. Thank you for believing in me. Thank you for your mentorship. It guided me along my path when I couldn't even see it beneath my feet. To Brandon, Chaunté, and Elizabeth, thank you. Thank you for sharing yourselves and your stories with me and in turn the readers of this book so openly. Thank you for being shining beacons of resilience. Thank you for being you. To Lisa, thank you. Thank you for your undying support. Thank you for your love. Thank you for every silly song and dance. You simply light me up and, in your heart, I have found home. Thank you to every individual who shared their story with the readers of this book. To every client, colleague, friend, acquaintance, and stranger with whom I've shared a smile and a laugh, thank you. Whether you know it or not, you were a part of my discovering this life's purpose. Thank you for allowing me to discover it through you.

ABOUT THE AUTHOR

Cassandra Worthy is founder and CEO of Change Enthusiasm Global, a boutique consulting firm, with a client base spanning the Fortune 500 and larger all over the world. Her firm's partnership is rooted in the practice and associated tools of Change Enthusiasm, invigorating, educating, and inspiring organizations, C-suite executives, and business associations alike going through significant change, disruption, and transformation. Cassandra received her B.S. in Chemical Engineering from Georgia Tech and spent nearly 15 years working within the Consumer Packaged Goods industry (CPG), predominantly at Procter & Gamble, leading organizations through multibillion-dollar acquisitions prior to founding her own firm. She is now sharing the valuable lessons learned and practical strategies created to enable individuals to become self-actualized toward growth through change.

www.cassandraworthy.com

Hay House Titles of Related Interest

THE SHIFT, the movie,
starring Dr. Wayne W. Dyer
(available as an online streaming video)
www.hayhouse.com/the-shift-movie

***

*HIGH PERFORMANCE HABITS: How Extraordinary People Become
That Way,* by Brendon Burchard

MOVE THE NEEDLE: Yarns from an Unlikely Entrepreneur,
by Shelley Brander

*TIME, MONEY, FREEDOM: 10 Simple Rules to Redefine What's
Possible and Radically Reshape Your Life,* by Ray and Jessica Higdon

*WHO NOT HOW: The Formula to Achieve Bigger Goals Through
Accelerating Teamwork,* by Dan Sullivan with Dr. Benjamin Hardy

*YOUR STAND IS YOUR BRAND: How Deciding Who to Be (NOT What
to Do) Will Revolutionize Your Business,* by Patrick Gentempo

All of the above are available at your local bookstore
or may be ordered by visiting:

Hay House USA: www.hayhouse.com®
Hay House Australia: www.hayhouse.com.au
Hay House UK: www.hayhouse.co.uk
Hay House India: www.hayhouse.co.in

All of the above are available at www.hayhouse.co.uk.

***

Write Your Book.
Grow Your Business.

AUTHORPRENEUR
MEMBERSHIP BY HAY HOUSE

Discover one of the best ways to **establish** your expertise, strategically **increase** your revenue, organically **attract** more customers, and **deliver** your message on a wider scale.

Wherever you are on the book-writing journey, our five-pathway process will meet you there. We walk with you step-by-step, from getting the book written—choosing your ideal reader, picking the best topic, outlining your material, and even finding professionals to help you—all the way through to publishing, launching, and keeping sales going.

JOIN HERE: WWW.HAYHOUSE.COM/APMEMBERSHIP

Let us show you how a book can help you reach your goals—no matter what type of business you're growing!

MEDITATE.
VISUALIZE.
LEARN.

Get the **Empower You**
Unlimited Audio *Mobile App*

Get unlimited access to the entire Hay House audio library!

You'll get:

- 500+ inspiring and life-changing **audiobooks**

- 200+ ad-free **guided meditations** for sleep, healing, relaxation, spiritual connection, and more

- Hundreds of audios **under 20 minutes** to easily fit into your day

- **Exclusive content** *only* for subscribers

- No credits, **no limits**

New audios added every week!

⭐⭐⭐⭐⭐ **I ADORE this app.**
I use it almost every day. Such a blessing. – Aya Lucy Rose

Scan me with **your phone camera!**

HAY HOUSE

TRY FOR FREE!
Go to: hayhouse.co.uk/listen-free

CONNECT WITH
HAY HOUSE
ONLINE

🌐 hayhouse.co.uk   **f** @hayhouse

📷 @hayhouseuk   🐦 @hayhouseuk

▶ @hayhouseuk   🎵 @hayhouseuk

Find out all about our latest books & card decks • Be the first to know about exclusive discounts • Interact with our authors in live broadcasts • Celebrate the cycle of the seasons with us • Watch free videos from your favourite authors • Connect with like-minded souls

'*The gateways to wisdom and knowledge are always open.*'

Louise Hay